HORNBY
magazine yearbook

Edited by Mike Wild

Ian Allan
PUBLISHING

CONTENTS

Editor: Mike Wild
Designer: Matt Chapman
Contributors: Andrew Roden, James Lavery, Phil Parker and Chris Nevard.

First published 2010
ISBN 978 0 7110 3530 0

An imprint of Ian Allan Publishing Ltd, Hersham, Surrey KT12 4RG.
Printed in England by Ian Allan Publishing Ltd, Hersham, Surrey KT12 4TG
Code: 1011/F1

Distributed in the United States of America and Canada by BookMasters Distribution Services

Visit the Ian Allan Publishing website at www.ianallanpublishing.com

A Stanier 'Princess Royal' thunders along the low level lines on the Warley Model Railway Club's Dalby Wood.
Trevor Jones.

Welcome

Welcome to the third *Hornby Magazine Yearbook* which is brought to you by the editorial team behind Ian Allan Publishing's *Hornby Magazine*. As always we've put together a feature packed edition filled with inspirational photographs, historical features and, most importantly, tips and techniques to help you get the most from your own projects.

We've also built a new layout to feature in this Yearbook, but, as a change of direction, it is an 'N' gauge project. The idea behind the new layout is to show just how much railway can be built in this scale using a modest 6ft x 4ft baseboard area and also to illustrate just how much the quality and detail of rolling stock has moved on for 'N'.

It has been a long time in coming for 'N' gauge. The European and American markets have historically always been 10 steps ahead in terms of detail and performance in this scale, but it is more than pleasing to be able to report that the British market is catching up very, very quickly. The latest offerings from the two main players in ready-to-run British 'N' have really been pushing the boundaries with this scale and they continue to do so too. Take a look through the catalogues of Bachmann's Graham Farish arm of Dapol and you'll soon see the potential for creating a miniature world in 'N'.

In the wider field the whole model railway market has continued to move forward progressively despite uncertain financial times and the manufacturers haven't rested on their laurels – in fact they have all been pushing forward with a number of projects both public and private which keeps the momentum of the hobby on a roll.

However, it isn't just the manufacturers which are driving the wants and needs of modellers – retailers are getting in on the game too.

Commissioning of exclusive ready-to-run models has risen dramatically this year following in the footsteps of Kernow Model Rail Centre's first commissions to Dapol in 2008. Now Rails of Sheffield, Hattons of Liverpool and Olivia's Trains from Sheffield are all working on their own unique projects with Bachmann and Dapol respectively and here at *Hornby Magazine* we are also in on the game working with Dapol to produce our own exclusive model of the LMS Stove R six-wheel passenger brake for 'OO' modellers.

The phrase 'you've never had it so good' is becoming something of a cliché in railway modelling circles, but it is also a statement which is becoming more and more true. Never before has the market been so buoyant, never before have there been so many new models in the course of production and I also think that the manufacturers are becoming increasingly committed to giving us, their customers, what we really want.

If you have just returned to the hobby doubtless you will be awestruck by the range of models and accessories which are available today and also the quality and I believe it is the same for those who have been constantly involved with it too. We really are getting the best from the hobby, its manufacturers and models and it is something we all want to see continue for generations to come.

Mike Wild

Mike Wild
Editor, *Hornby Magazine*
Peterborough, August 2010

Hornby Magazine's **new 'N' gauge layout makes its debut in this book on pages 18-27. A Dapol BR '9F' 2-10-0 leads a string of loaded bogie bolster wagons through Hettle.** Mike Wild.

On Western metals

2010 marked the 175th anniversary of the Great Western Railway and it remains a popular subject for modellers of all eras. Here we look at five of the layouts which have captured the varying spirit of God's Wonderful Railway.

Penrhos

What better setting is there for a Great Western Railway-built branch line than the rolling hills of Wales? This magnificent layout called Penrhos has been built by Dave Spencer with more than a little inspiration from Pendon Museum and the work of master model maker Roye England.

However, rather than being a pure Great Western branch, the layout turns the clock forward to the 1950s and 1960s and makes the most of the mix of ex-GWR and ex-LMS motive power which served areas of rural Wales in the final two decades of steam.

At just 12ft long and 18in wide Penrhos offers a wonderful landscape in a very modest space. As well as the station, goods yard and locomotive shed it also features a quarry at one end and sidings for an engineering works at the other. These latter two features also disguise the fiddle yards where trains are prepared and despatched for their journey through Penrhos.

Penrhos statistics	
Builder:	Dave Spencer
Scale:	'OO'
Length:	12ft
Width:	18in
Track:	Peco Code 75
Period:	BR Western Region, 1950s-1960s
Featured:	HM24

Construction of this layout saw Dave make many trips to Wales to record the types of vegetation seen by the lineside and also research building styles. At the same time rolling stock was being built and developed and while the majority of the locomotives are ready-to-run items, the wagon fleet is extensively kit built, offering a greater taste of the variety of goods vehicles which once operated on Britain's railways in the 1950s.

It might not be on the same scale as Pendon's magnificent Vale Scene, but Penrhos surely is a microcosm of rural Wales as it was in the later days of steam.

An ex-GWR '4575' waits in the loop at Penrhos before moving to the shed for coal and water. Chris Nevard.

A '57XX' 0-6-0PT shunts the brake van for the next departure of loaded stone wagons from the quarry. Chris Nevard.

Viewed across the fields on the approach to Penrhos a '45XX' 2-6-2T approaches with the local stopping service. Chris Nevard.

A 'Castle' approaches
Kingsfield on the GWR
lines with an express.
Mike Wild.

Kingsfield

You could be forgiven for thinking that all Western Region layouts are based on branch line operations because there have been so many on the exhibition circuit past and present. However, Kingsfield by the Barnhill Model Railway Club is no branch line. At 25ft x 9ft 8in this monster main line set is one not to miss.

The layout was started in 1999 and 11 years later the small team behind it are still enjoying exhibiting and maintaining it for thousands to enjoy. When it was started Kingsfield was a break from the norm for the Barnhill club as previous layouts had all been based around terminus to fiddle yard operations. The continuous run design chosen for Kingsfield has allowed a greater variety of

stock to be operated as well as scale length trains representing Western, Midland and Southern Region traffic.

The theory behind the operations comes from observations on an old railway map which showed two lines that didn't interlink but equally, if the companies had seen fit, could have. Both were within the Western Region boundary with possible links to the Midlands. These two routes were from Oxford to Fairford and Swindon to Highworth. By adding fictional links the result was a connection to the London Midland network and the Southern Region at Lambourn allowing a truly multi-regional context to be created for the fictitious station.

Even so, it is Western Region operated stock which dominates the

scene and one which is further dominated away from the railway by large industrial structures and the impressive terminus and through station of Kingsfield. Add to this a large double junction radiating lines to the Midland/Southern and Western routes and an impressively large locomotive shed with a fully operational turntable and this layout has it all.

No transition era Western Region layout would be complete without the diesel hydraulics. A 'Warship' crosses into the through platforms. Mike Wild.

Kingsfield statistics	
Owner:	Barnhill MRC
Scale:	'00'
Length:	25 feet
Width:	9ft 8in
Track:	Peco
Period:	1950s/early 1960s
Featured:	HM30

A 'WD' 2-8-0 passes through the complex junction outside Kingsfield station as a 'Castle' waits patiently for a clear road with an express. Mike Wild.

Melcombe Magna

The Somerset & Dorset Railway might not seem like an obvious choice for a Western Region theme, but the associated branch lines saw ex-GWR locomotives working alongside Midland and Southern designs too.

Mike Baker's Melcombe Magna is a wonderful portrayal of the S&D in the 1950s and makes the most of the potential to operate locomotives and rolling stock from three of the five BR regions. It is built in 'O' gauge and occupies 20ft x 10ft 6in in a permanent setup which also includes a quarry railway.

The mixture of local passenger and goods trains, motive power and apparent slow pace of life all attracted Mike to the S&D as the subject for his layout and Melcombe Magna is the result of 12 years' work. Rather than model a specific location Mike used his favourite parts of the network to assemble a feasible and realistic setting which could quite easily have been part of the network. Melcombe Magna is a fictional town in mid-Dorset with extensive lime deposits nearby and the railway as an economical means of transport which competed effectively with the roads and canals of the day by offering quicker journey times.

The fictional history sees the branch from Melcombe Magna meet the S&D main line at Stalbridge Junction and trains for the branch run to Templecombe.

All the locomotives for Melcombe Magna, and rolling stock, are kit built and feature traditional S&D locomotives such as the ex-GWR '2251' 0-6-0 and '8750' 0-6-0PT as well as Midland and Southern designed machines allocated to Templecombe shed.

Without a doubt Melcombe Magna has a truly wonderful atmosphere which parallels the feeling of the Somerset & Dorset as we all like to remember it – charming and full of antiquity.

In scene which typifies the era, a '2251' 0-6-0 draws into the station with the passenger service.
Chris Nevard.

Melcombe Magna statistics	
Owner:	Mike Baker
Scale:	'O' and 16.5mm narrow gauge
Length:	20ft
Width:	10ft 6in
Track:	Handbuilt plus C&L finescale and Peco
Period:	Somerset and Dorset, BR 1950s
Featured:	HM31

An ex-GWR 0-6-0PT
arrives at Melcombe
Magna with the daily
mixed goods.
Chris Nevard.

Trenance

The Royal Duchy was the inspiration behind this evocation of North Cornwall in the changeover years from steam to diesel traction. Trenance is in fact a fictional joint British Railways Western Region/Southern Region terminus on the North Cornwall coast between Newquay and Padstow.

In the imaginary history the Cornwall Mineral Railways (CMR) built a line from Saint Dennis Junction (known as Bodmin Road Junction originally) in 1885 which enabled it to expand its routes to tap additional china clay resources. As the Great Western Railway (GWR) had been operating the CMR routes since 1877, it also operated the Trenance branch.

Close by the North Cornwall Railway (supported by the London & South Western Railway) had completed its Padstow branch in 1899 and was looking to extend further west. A branch was built in 1901 climbing fiercely out of Wadebridge to Trenance. This new route met the original GWR route two miles outside Trenance at a junction called Retorick Junction.

The track layout was influenced by the original requirement to run large locomotives and five-coach trains and replicate prototype practice where possible. A detailed timetable has been created to reflect Friday, Saturday and Sunday operations in the peak summer period offering a myriad of movements through the highly effective and flexible track layout which forms the entrance to Trenance station.

As well as the station, builder Nigel Mann has included a locomotive servicing depot with a turntable, goods yard and Royal Navy fuel depot, all of which add to the overall entertainment value both for the operators and the viewing public alike.

After 10 years Trenance is now becoming a regular fixture of the model railway exhibition circuit, but by Nigel's own admission it took much longer to complete than expected. The end result though is a working railway with historical and accurate operations which capture a might-have-been station in one of the finest areas of the country.

Trenance statistics	
Owner:	Nigel Mann
Scale:	'OO'
Length:	12ft
Width:	15ft
Track:	Peco code 100
Period:	1960s, Western and Southern Region
Featured:	HM35

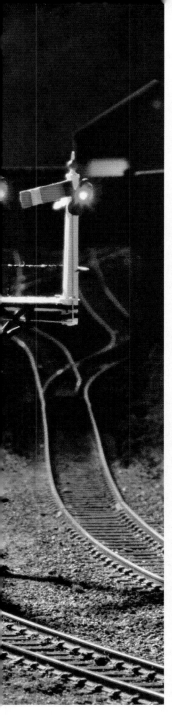

In the cold night air a '4575' and '2251' pass outside the locomotive depot at Trenance.
Trevor Jones.

The depot at Trenance is kept busy turning and preparing locomotives for the packed timetable.
Trevor Jones.

Llangenydd

The railways of Wales are a popular subject for model projects and Ken Jones' Llangenydd offers another superb example of this. The North Wales-based model was originally started by fellow High Wycombe & District Model Railway Society member Ron North, but with too many projects on his hands he passed it over to its current owner Ken.

Since then the scenery has been completed with additional details and a new fleet of rolling stock representing both Western and Midland prototypes has been assembled to develop the layout for exhibition and home use.

Llangenydd is not a real place, but a fictional terminus situated just inland from the Lleyn Peninsula coastline on the remains of the ex-Cambrian Railway branch to Llantwp which uses mainly ex-GWR motive power. To complete the picture an ex-LMS branch runs along the North coast and joins the Llantwp branch at Twpsin Junction which allows trains from both regions to be operated to Llangenydd. The main traffic on the line is for the Army and RAF training camps and latterly construction traffic for a hydro-electric power station.

The layout is compact at 9ft 6in x 18in including a sector plate fiddle yard, but nevertheless it incorporates plenty of operational features as well as scenic details. The scenic side of Llangenydd has been enhanced by Ken's eye for detail which has included adding cameos such as a flock of sheep holding up the local bus service, appropriately decorated and positioned road vehicles and personnel and more.

Llangenydd statistics

Owner:	Ken Jones
Scale:	'OO'
Length:	9ft 6in
Width:	18in
Track:	Peco code 75
Period:	BR 1950s, Western Region
Featured:	HM37

A Collett '2251' arrives at Llangenydd in a classic scene from North Wales in the 1950s. Chris Nevard.

Both Western and Midland locomotives operate into Llangenydd. A Swindon built Ivatt '2MT' 2-6-0 pauses in the platform as a '4575' shunts the goods yard. Chris Nevard.

The
6ft main line

How do you squeeze a quart into a pint pot? Downscale to 'N' gauge is the answer! **MIKE WILD** reveals the story behind this new 'N' gauge layout built by *Hornby Magazine* to show just how much potential 2mm scale holds to today's layout builder. *Photography, Mike Wild.*

Why? That was the most common question I was asked while discussing this new layout. Not because I was planning yet another layout build, but because I was developing an idea for an 'N' gauge layout. And my response... why not!

I think the real reason that the question of 'why' emerged so many times is that British 'N' became something of a misnomer in the late 1990s except for serious modellers, but in the past decade since Bachmann took over the former Graham Farish brand and Dapol entered the ready-to-run market for the scale general perceptions have been changed, although there are undoubtedly some who still need persuading of the potential of this scale. Change the timescale to the past five years and there is an even greater lift in the quality, performance and availability of 'N' gauge rolling stock which continues as both Bachmann and Dapol strive to produce ever more reliable and detailed models.

As a modeller I always was an 'N' gauge person, starting at the tender age of 7. My first layout developed and grew as my pocket money allowed and ultimately resulted in a rabbit warren trackplan which had more facets than many of today's exhibition layouts – although I'm more than happy to admit that the scenery left something to be desired! Still it served its purpose and allowed me to develop a railway in a space which otherwise would have probably resulted in a branch line in any other scale. Things have changed since then. I've had an exhibition layout in 'N', sold it on, changed to 'OO' gauge and built five further layouts (although only three of those have been completed) and now, almost 10 years since I last seriously modelled in this scale I'm back, but with a new vision and more skills.

Many homes are short of space for a model railway, so I came up with an idea which revolved around a now traditional train set size baseboard measuring 6ft x 4ft. In 'OO' gauge it doesn't offer the potential I would personally want in terms of train lengths and realistic scenery, but in 'N' gauge the story is completely different.

When I started planning the criteria was singular – to be able to run near scale length passenger and goods trains. As a secondary I also wanted to develop a theme which could be operated in both the BR steam/diesel transition period and the BR corporate blue era covering the 1970s.

My original vision was quite conservative – a double track main line, a small through station and possibly a goods yard with a fiddle yard to the rear with, maybe, three tracks in each direction. That was until I started planning seriously and saw the true potential of what I thought could be achieved in the space available.

The trackplan which developed has been designed to make the most of the railway and scenery. It features a double track main line, a goods loop, a branch line, a cattle dock, a goods yard with a headshunt and acres of space for scenic modelling away from the railway.

Through the 4ft width of the baseboards I've been able to include four tracks in the fiddle yard in each direction for the main lines plus three sidings to serve the branch – in real numbers that's space for a minimum of 11 trains, or, if two of each of the four track groups is

BR '9F' 92100 approaches Hettle station with a loaded steel train as 'Crab' 42765 heads the other way with loaded 16-ton mineral wagons.

The Eastern Region's roster is growing with Dapol's 'B17' and soon to be released 'B1' 4-6-0s, but the real winner in terms of the steam/diesel transition era is the London Midland Region.

Bachmann has championed this area with its Stanier designed models covering the 'Jubilee', rebuilt 'Royal Scot' and 'Black Five' plus there are also reasonable models of the Stanier '8F', Fowler '4F', Hughes-Fowler 'Crab and 'Jinty' in the Graham Farish range which with a little bufferbeam detail and a good weathering job can be lifted considerably from their factory finish. Add to this Dapol's delightful Ivatt '2MT' 2-6-2T, '9F' 2-10-0 and the newly released 'Britannia' 4-6-2 and the range of steam models is quite considerable.

All this lead me towards another ambition – to create a model based on that most wonderful of scenic railways, the Settle and Carlisle line through the Northern fells. In my view no other railway journey in England can match it for the sheer drama and when you look back at photographs of the route in the 1950s and 1960s it oozes atmosphere.

As you might expect 6ft x 4ft didn't allow for me to model an exact replica of one of the stations, but it has given me enough space to create an impression of the S&C. The station buildings were another catalyst, based on Dent station on the S&C, and are from Hornby's Lyddle End 'N' gauge building range. In fact the Lyddle End range has provided all nine of

A BR Sulzer Type 2 ambles towards Hettle from the branch with empty 'Dogfish' ballast hoppers.

A Hughes-Fowler 'Crab' 2-6-0 passes through the countryside surrounding Hettle with a mixed goods.

used to its two train capacity, 14 trains. Just as importantly it can handle near scale length trains with nine coach passenger trains and 25 wagons goods being the upper limit – impressive for such a small area.

An important part of the scenic section for me was to include realistic curves, so these have been carefully planned and curved gently to sweep through the scenery making full use of the 4ft wide baseboards. This has also made the size of the baseboards less obvious as the railway

hardly has any straights on it – the only straight areas being in the goods yard.

Midland vision

Admittedly at the moment choices for an 'N' gauge layout using mainly new rolling stock are a little limited. The Southern has fared well with Dapol's 'M7' 0-4-4T, 'Q1' 0-6-0 and 'Terrier' 0-6-0T, but these models are only backed up by now comparatively dated models of the Bulleid 'West Country' and 'Merchant Navy' from Bachmann's Graham Farish stable.

the buildings which grace the layout covering a farm estate, station buildings, goods yard and signalbox.

Construction started with the baseboards which are of the conventional solid top design. The tops are cut from 9mm plywood and are kept rigid by 3in x 1in timber framing around the edges with two cross braces in between the ends. To support the layout four trestles were built with 3in x 1in timber using metal hinges at the tops to allow them to fold out and metal chain between the lower braces to stop the legs spreading too far apart and the layout collapsing.

Having worked in 'OO' gauge for so long it took me a while to readjust to 'N' gauge and particularly in terms of track geometry. I already knew that I didn't want any curves tighter than second radius so one of the first items I bought was a tracksetta gauge for 10 ½in radius curves. The whole layout has been laid with Peco code 55 flexible track. All the points are live frog consisting of mainly large radius and a smattering of medium radius points. Most of the points in the fiddle yard are curved large radius points which have allowed the sidings to be lengthened to their maximum potential. Although a little unconventional, I opted not to add underlay beneath the track.

Having laid the track it was all thoroughly test run with a variety of trains to ensure that everything was as it should

be. Next the copper clad strips were cut to length and added at the baseboard joins followed by the rails being soldered to them ready for the two baseboards to be parted at a future date. Wire droppers were also added at this stage for all the track electrical connections before proceeding to the next stage.

The whole layout is analogue controlled with a control panel located to one side of the fiddle yard.

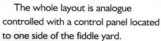

The farm has been detailed with vehicles, dogs and more to bring it to life.

BR 'Britannia' 70000 *Britannia* (Dapol's latest 'N' gauge steam locomotive) thunders through Hettle with an express and passes with a 'Black Five' 4-6-0 at the head of a rake of box vans.

Three Gaugemaster handheld controllers are used and connect to the layout through four pin DIN plugs being split between the two main lines and the branch line/goods yard with switching between controllers to allow smooth control of trains between sections. The points on the scenic section are operated by DCC Concepts new Cobalt point

motors operated through centre sprung toggle switches while the fiddle yard point motors are Peco surface mounted motors controlled by the same type of switch but powered by a capacitor discharge unit.

Rather than working my way through painting the rail sides by hand I took my now usual option of spray painting the rails, sleepers and baseboard surface by

first masking off the fiddle yard area completely and secondly by masking each of the point blades with 10mm wide masking tape. This meant that the Railmatch frame dirt spray paint could be applied directly over the track, left to dry then cleaned off and still allow perfect running when the trains returned.

Developing the scenery

Scenery can make or break a layout and I was determined to get it right with this layout having viewed my previous efforts at 'N' gauge scenery as being rather less than what I felt I could achieve now. I've also been able to use the techniques I've developed over the last couple of years with Bay Street Shed Mk II and more recently Berrybridge.

The difficult part, or what I perceived to be difficult, was scaling the scenery to suit 'N' gauge, but once I got started I realised that virtually every technique I'd used on my 'OO' layouts could be transferred to this smaller scale project.

The starting point was to create a scheme for the placing of roads and buildings. Roads were easy – I knew I wanted a road bridge as a scenic break at each end of the layout, rather than tunnels – so a scheme was drawn out on the baseboard with a felt tip pen to act as a guide for further development.

An '8F' leads a long rake of loaded 16-ton mineral wagons through Hettle as a Class 108 slows for the station stop.

With this planned I needed to devise a way of installing a bridge at the 'country' end. The station end was easy, as I'd already decided to use a Hornby Lyddle End road overbridge modelled in stone, but the country end was more difficult as whatever I decided upon had to cross three tracks. The final version revolves around Peco girder bridge sides with bridge parapets made from thick card covered with Slater's embossed 'N' gauge brick plasticard.

The scenic contours have been built up from both double thickness corrugated cardboard and foamboard as required to create a smooth but interesting terrain which includes a flat area for the farm estate. The contour height was chosen to reflect the rising terrain of the Northern fells, but equally I'd viewed this layout as being set in the lower lying areas where the grass grows lush and green during the spring and summer so there are no giant mountains in this scene. I've also aimed to set the railway into a shallow, but more than likely man made, cutting where the scenery slops in from all sides to the railway. This has allowed the scenery around the railway at the very front of the

board to be near flat allowing a good view of the trains as they pass through.

With contours created the roads were cut from thick card and glued in place on top followed by a web of masking tape to cover the whole of the

scenic area. On top of this squares of newspaper were glued in place with PVA glue to create a hard wearing but light skin onto which the ground cover could be added. Once it was dry, the railway and fiddle yard were masked and

A Bachmann Graham Farish 'Royal Scot' 4-6-0 leads a rake of BR maroon Stanier stock towards Hettle station.

'N' gauge 6ft mailn line track plan

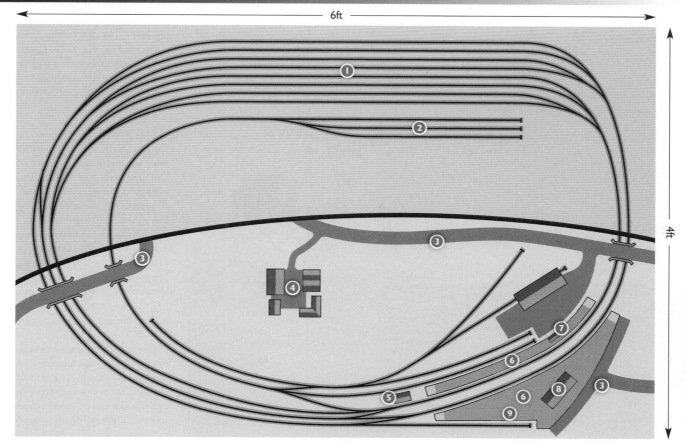

← 6ft →

4ft

① Fiddle yard	④ Farm	⑦ Waiting room
② Branch line fiddle yard	⑤ Signalbox	⑧ Station building
③ Roads	⑥ Platform	⑨ Cattle dock

A BR Sulzer 'Peak' Type 4 passes through Hettle with an express as a Class 108 DMU departs with the branch service.

the whole layout was then spray painted with dark brown to give a dark base colour to the future layers of ground cover.

With all this done it was a case of developing the platforms and coming up with a way to make realistic textured road surfaces. The platforms have a foamboard formwork which is then covered with Slater's embossed 'N' gauge brick plasticard for the platform faces and hand scribed cardboard for the surface which has been made to represent a stone paving.

For the roads I hit upon the idea of using Greenscene's textured paints and chose their light tarmac colour for the main roads which worked a treat. The goods yard was treated to a cobbled finish (together with the station approach and cattle dock area) which was then painted with Humbrol acrylic

No. 64 for a light stone finish and weathered with Carrs weathering powders.

The track has been ballasted with a 3:1 mixture of Woodland Scenics fine grey and light grey ballasts respectively glued in place with diluted PVA glue applied with a syringe.

Going green

The grass has been built up in several layers, but it all started out with the farm estate and the idea for a ploughed field. Here I took the opportunity to use Tamiya's texture paints and used the dark earth colour for both the field and the centre of the farm and approach road. While the paint was still wet Woodland Scenics blended green turf was sprinkled down the centre of the approach road and scattered lightly at random over small areas of the ploughed field to represent new grass growing through.

Next the rest of the layout was treated to a coat of Woodland Scenic fine turf consisting of a mixture of the blended green and blended earth colour mixes. The only area which used the blended green turf singularly was the garden of the farm house which is intended to represent a well tended lawn.

At this point the layout's scenery was looking very uniform and while I knew what I wanted to achieve I wasn't sure that the method I had in mind was going

With a stopping train formed of suburban stock, a BR '3MT' 2-6-2T approaches Hettle from the branch.

Table 1 – Materials and manufacturers

Product	Manufacturer	Product	Manufacturer
Blended green fine turf	Woodland Scenics	Winter 4.5mm static grass	miniNatur
Blended earth fine turf	Woodland Scenics	Winter 6mm static grass	miniNatur
Light green coarse turf	Woodland Scenics	Midland signalbox	Hornby Lyddle End
Polyfibre	Woodland Scenics	Midland station building	Hornby Lyddle End
Fine grey ballast	Woodland Scenics	Midland waiting room	Hornby Lyddle End
Fine light grey ballast	Woodland Scenics	Midland Goods shed	Hornby Lyddle End
Field grass, hay	Woodland Scenics	Farm house	Hornby Lyddle End
Sycamore trees (large)	Woodland Scenics	Barn	Hornby Lyddle End
Sycamore trees (small)	Woodland scenics	Plough shed	Hornby Lyddle end
Oak trees (large)	Woodland Scenics	Tractor shed	Hornby Lyddle End
Oak trees (small)	Woodland Scenics	Road overbridge	Hornby Lyddle end
Walnut trees (large)	Woodland Scenics	Cattle dock	Hornby Lyddle End
Willow tree	The Model Tree Shop	Spear fencing	Ratio
Fruit tree	The Model Tree Shop	Lineside fencing	Ratio
Blossom tree	The Model Tree Shop	Pallets, sacks and barrels	Ratio
Beech tree	The Model Tree Shop	Girder bridges	Peco
Etched brass trees	The Model Tree Shop	Code 55 track	Peco
Light tarmac textured paint	Greenscene	Surface mounted point motor	Peco
Soil effect textured paint	Tamiya	Cobalt point motor	DCC Concepts
LMS lattice post stop signal	P&D Marsh	Brick embossed plasticard	Slaters
LMS two post bracket signal	P&D Marsh	Random stone embossed plasticard	Slaters
LMS three post bracket signal	P&D Marsh	Period adverts	Pre-cut station signs
LMS home and distant signal	P&D Marsh	Cows	Noch
LMS ground signals	P&D Marsh	Cats and dogs	Noch
LMS station lamps	P&D Marsh	People	Noch
Victorian gents toilet	P&D Marsh	Flower boxes	Adrian's Ideas/Buffers Model Railways
Autumn 4.5mm static grass	miniNatur		

to work! What I had planned was static grass and what I planned, in my eyes at least, has worked a treat. At first I thought that the 4.5mm and 6mm long static fibres I had in stock from Bay Street and Berrybridge would be too long, but as I added more to the layout it became clear that they were the right choice to represent long untended grass.

Using a mixture of autumn and winter coloured miniNatur static grass fibres the whole layout received its second coat of colour and this was embellished further at the time by sprinkling the mixture of Woodland Scenic's blended green and earth turfs into the wet glue underneath the static grass adding depth and texture at the same time.

After drying overnight it was clear that more texture was needed so I returned to another of my 'stock' methods – employing a can of Railmatch matt varnish, Woodland Scenic's blended green and earth fine turfs plus Woodland Scenic's light green coarse turf. To work with these materials an A4 sized scrap of cardboard was used as a mask to stop the matt varnish straying where I didn't want it while the spray was directed at the grass areas. As soon as the varnish had been applied the various turfs were sprinkled, spread and worked into the static grass at random to create a more visually pleasing layout with lots of texture, tone and variety of hue.

The hedges have been created by teasing out Woodland Scenic polyfibre into long thin strips, spraying with Railmatch frame dirt from an aerosol and sprinkling with a mixture of Woodland Scenic's blended turfs to give them a variety of colour and tone. Once dry these were further stretched to reduce their height before being glued in place with PVA glue.

To populate the layout further I wanted to add plenty of trees, and not just small trees. Around half a dozen of the trees are from the Model Tree shop including the blossoming bush at the back of the farm, the apple tree in the farm house garden and the willow tree on the edge of the farm. All the remaining trees are from Woodlands Scenic's premium tree range, some as supplied others with a hint of extra texture and colouring through the use of more of those wonderful blended fine turfs and coarse turfs.

The final detailing

With a layout at this stage it is easy to think it can be viewed as finished, but the smart and textured canvas also presents the opportunity for detailing. The first area to be tackled was the signalling. All of the signals used on the layout were supplied ready assembled by P&D Marsh and are of LMS pattern. These suit the layout perfectly and were a joy to install,

especially as they were pre-assembled. The package also included five ground signals which have been used for the goods yard, cattle dock siding and crossover. The bracket signal controlling access to the main line and goods loop on the outer loop has been modified by swapping the two posts over to give priority to the main line.

Fencing has been added around the platform using Ratio spear fencing which is superbly moulded and required very little effort to add to the layout. Further fencing has been added around the goods yard using Ratio lineside fencing spray painted with Railmatch sleeper grime and glued in place with super glue. The station has also had lamps from P&D Marsh painted in London Midland Region

Suppliers

Woodland Scenics	www.bachmann.co.uk
Graham Farish (Bachmann)	www.bachmann.co.uk
Dapol	www.dapol.co.uk
P&D Marsh	www.pdmarshmodels.co.uk
The Model Tree Shop	www.themodeltreeshop.co.uk
Hornby (Lyddle End)	www.hornby.com
Greenscene	www.green-scene.co.uk
Noch (via Gaugemaster)	www.gaugemaster.com
Slaters Plastikard	www.slatersplastikard.com
DCC Concepts	www.dccconcepts.com
International Models (miniNatur)	www.internationalmodels.net
Ratio	www.peco-uk.com
Adrian's Ideas	www.buffersmodelrailways.co.uk

A Stanier 'Jubilee' passes through Hettle with an express formed of Stanier Period III coaches.

crimson added to the platforms together with flower boxes from Adrian's Ideas – although the latter are intended for 'OO' they look the part on the station. People are by Noch and if you look closely you'll also see the station cat, packing cases and a few other little touches.

The station area also features a cattle dock which has been added by cutting the base off the Hornby Lyddle End cattle dock and fixing it directly to the cobbled stone surface. Inside the pen has been detailed with cut down lengths of Woodland Scenic's hay coloured field

grass onto which a small number of Noch cows have been added to complete the scene.

In the goods yard a few extra details have been added including a disused yard crane minus its lifting hook and rope, a scratch built coal staithe built up

HOW TO DO IT Building the 6ft main line

1 Track is from Peco's code 55 range. During an early testing session an '8F' leads a coal train past the signalbox.

2 At the baseboard joints copperclad board has been laid with the rails soldered to it to form a strong and resilient join when the layout is in transport.

3 The scenic areas trackwork was spray painted with Railmatch sleeper grime to give it a weathered effect. The point blades were masked with 10mm wide masking tape while the fiddle yard was covered with a clear dust sheet.

4 The platforms are built on a form work of foamboard together with the rest of the scenery.

5 The right hand scenic break is formed of a bridge over the main lines and a tunnel for the branch line. The bridge sides are from the Peco range.

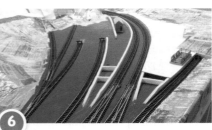

6 The scenic surface is built from small squares of newspaper glued in place with PVA glue and built up in layers. The finished surface is strong and light.

from layers of Slater's wood planking embossed plasticard, spray painted with Railmatch weathered black and filled with Woodland Scenics mine run coal. Further details include pallets, sacks of coal and oil drums from the Ratio range and a selection of boxes and chains from my everlasting 'N' gauge spares box!

Table 1 lists all of the scenic products and their manufacturer used in this layout.

Rolling stock

No layout would be complete without rolling stock and this one is no exception! The stock roster is drawn entirely from Bachmann's Graham Farish and the Dapol ranges although there are a handful of kits nearing completion of reworking after dragging them out of store for a revamp.

Highlights amongst the rolling stock fleet include a rake of 24 16-ton mineral wagons, all loaded with coal and weathered, a rake of bogie bolster wagons loaded with steel beams, a rebuilt 'Royal Scot' hauled rake of BR maroon Stanier stock and a host of other trains. Table 2 lists the locomotives available for the layout. Naturally this will undoubtedly expand over the coming months prior to the layouts exhibition debut in 2011.

All the rolling stock has been weathered to some lesser or greater extent. All the locomotives and carriages have been weathered with

Lifecolor Railway Weathering paints through an airbrush while the wagons are both airbrush and powder weathered.

The future

Like any layout, I'm sure this one isn't really finished. I'll always find another detail to add, something to change or a new item of rolling stock to add. In fact just a couple of days after finishing the layout I was already considering adding a 6in extension to front to increase the scenic depth further – but that as they say, is another story.

■ This layout has been sponsored by Woodland Scenic's and built with the support of Graham Farish, P&D Marsh, Greenscene and the Model Tree Shop which we would like to thank for all their contributions. Without them it would never have been finished!

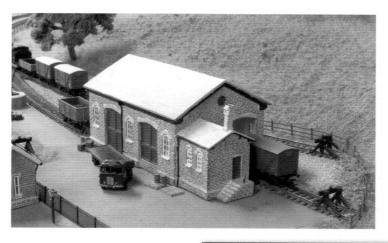

The goods shed is kept busy with arriving and departing wagon loads.

Table 2 – Stock roster	
Locomotive	**Manufacturer**
Hughes-Fowler 'Crab' 2-6-0	Bachmann/Graham Farish
Fowler 'Jinty' 0-6-0T	Bachmann/Graham Farish
Fowler '4F' 0-6-0	Bachmann/Graham Farish
Stanier 'Jubilee' 4-6-0	Bachmann/Graham Farish
Stanier 'Royal Scot' 4-6-0	Bachmann/Graham Farish
Stanier 'Black Five' 4-6-0	Bachmann/Graham Farish
Stanier '8F' 2-8-0	Bachmann/Graham Farish
Ivatt '2MT' 2-6-2T	Dapol
BR '3MT' 2-6-2T	Bachmann/Graham Farish
BR '4MT' 2-6-4T	Bachmann/Graham Farish
BR '7MT' 4-6-2	Dapol
BR '9F' 2-10-0	Dapol
English Electric Type 3	Bachmann/Graham Farish
Sulzer Type 2	Bachmann/Graham Farish
Brush Type 4	Bachmann/Graham Farish
Sulzer Type 4	Bachmann/Graham Farish
Brush Type 3	Bachmann/Graham Farish
Derby two-car DMU	Bachmann/Graham Farish
Derby three-car DMU	Bachmann/Graham Farish

7 Once all of the scenic area was covered with newspaper over the masking tape web, the whole area was spray painted with a dark brown. The tracks and platforms were masked to maintain their already weathered state.

8 Grass work developed around the farm estate. To create the soil effect Tamiya textured paints were used with Woodland Scenic's blended green fine turf sprinkled on randomly.

9 The final platform surface is scribed 2mm thick cardboard with platform edging being strips of Slaters' brick embossed plasticard.

10 The grass has been built up in layers. First was a covering of Woodland Scenics fine blended green and earth turfs followed by this, a second layer of miniNatur autumn and winter static grasses to give the surface greater depth.

11 The cattle dock is from Hornby's Lyddle End range with the cast resin base removed. It was further detailed with hay and cows.

12 Signals from P&D Marsh add character to the railway scene together with grass growing through the ballast in selected areas.

Recreating God's
Wonderful
Railway

To mark the 175th anniversary of the Great Western Railway, **Andrew Roden** looks back at the company's fascinating history and considers how it can be modelled.

For many years the Great Western Railway (GWR) branch line terminus was something of a modelling cliché but ironically, this legendary company which gave us the 'Kings', 'Castles' and 'Halls' – alongside the smaller but equally important pannier and prairie tanks – started off as a high-speed main line from Bristol to London and only later became known for its rural routes.

The GWR has appealed ever since Isambard Kingdom Brunel persuaded the company's directors to omit any mention of the railway's gauge from the Act of Parliament which it obtained on August 31 1835. Brunel's resulting 7ft 0¼in broad gauge differentiated the GWR from the very start and helped establish a reputation for speed and performance in the early days which standard gauge rivals

could barely approach, let alone exceed. The first trains ran in 1838, and by 1841 were running to Bristol over the Great Western Main Line and onwards to Exeter over the allied Bristol & Exeter Railway.

From then until the end of the 1860s is what might be called the first phase of the GWR. Although the first steam locomotives were with one important

exception unreliable and badly performing freaks, the company's first Locomotive Superintendent, Daniel Gooch, soon applied lessons from the 2-2-2 *North Star* to a range of locomotives built at the new railway works in Swindon from the mid 1840s. Even though the broad gauge was quickly recognised to be a handicap, the GWR expanded through acquisitions and alliances until by the time the Royal Albert Bridge at Saltash, Cornwall, opened in 1859, the GWR's empire extended from Paddington to Falmouth, South West Wales and as far north as Chester.

It wasn't all broad gauge however, as the railway to the West Midlands had been built with dual gauge tracks and north of Wolverhampton the GWR was standard gauge as Parliament forbade the exclusive use of the broad gauge on the Oxford and Birmingham, and Birmingham, Wolverhampton and Dudley Railways while the Shrewsbury and Birmingham, and Shrewsbury and Chester railways were standard gauge from the outset.

The transition years

The acquisition of the West Midland Railway (a merged company of the Oxford Worcester and Wolverhampton, Worcester and Hereford, and Newport and Abergavenny railways) in 1861 saw the gradual transition of the GWR from broad to standard gauge. With greater access to new markets in the Midlands and Wales, standard gauge rails were gradually extended south, reaching Paddington in 1861. However, the GWR suffered greatly in the 1860s. First, Gooch departed as Locomotive Superintendent in 1864, and then the GWR overreached itself financially to the point of seeking an emergency loan from government (which was refused). Only when Gooch returned in a new role as chairman was the ship steadied and the new Chief Mechanical Engineer Joseph Armstrong given funds to start the lengthy process of transforming the GWR into the railway we are familiar with.

Gooch finally recognised the weakness of the broad gauge and from the early 1870s exclusively broad gauge routes such as the South Wales Railway were converted to standard gauge in a gradual process that continued through the 1870s and 1880s. Further mergers and takeovers took place throughout this period, the most important being the GWR gaining ownership of the railways from Exeter to Penzance after a failed attempt to buy the Somerset & Dorset Railway. It meant the GWR had a secure wedge of territory running West from Paddington in which competition was limited, with the notable exception of the London & South Western Railway's routes into North Cornwall.

Joseph Armstrong's locomotive designs have long passed into memory but some lasted many years – the last of his famous '517' 0-4-2Ts of 1868 was not withdrawn until 1945. Armstrong was succeeded in 1877 by William Dean, who had the daunting task of providing new locomotives and carriages which could be converted from broad to standard gauge as the standard of much of the broad gauge rolling stock was by this time very poor. Dean produced some of the GWR's most important locomotives ever, from the '3031' 2-2-2s (soon altered to 4-2-2s after a derailment in Box Tunnel) to the 'Dean Goods' 0-6-0s of 1883, which not only ran until the 1950s but also showed up the London Midland & Scottish

The GWR 'Castle' class 4-6-0s became a symbol of the GWR with production continuing through three decades into the 1950s. Early in its career 4076 *Carmarthen Castle* passes under Skewen arches with the 3.55pm Swansea-London Paddington express in 1929.

Frank Hebron/Rail Archive Stephenson.

Express trains may have been in the public eye for the GWR, but freight was equally important to the company's survival – and especially in South Wales where lucrative coal mines generated heavy rail traffic. Ex-GWR '56XX' 0-6-2T 5698 passes Newport with a down train of coal empties on March 4 1961. Bob Tuck/Rail Archive Stephenson.

Railway's post-war '2MT' 2-6-0s under test!

With the conversion of the Truro-Exeter route from broad to standard gauge in 1892, the stage was set for a radical transformation of a railway which until this point had been regarded as slow and conservative since the 1860s. The period from 1892 to the Great War in 1914 would finally see the GWR regain and retain its 'Great' prefix.

Rebirth

The final abolition of the broad gauge unshackled the GWR from its past. Dynamic leadership in commercial and engineering spheres backed by the company's rising profitability created a perfect storm which allowed the railway to first match and then exceed all of its counterparts in mainland Britain.

The rebirth began with the opening of the Severn Tunnel in 1886, which cut Bristol to Cardiff journey times by up to 90 minutes by virtue of cutting off the previously lengthy route via Gloucester. The tunnel took 13 years to build and cost a fortune, but its value was immense, as it increased capacity on the route from South Wales to London, though at the time all trains had to negotiate Bristol's

increasingly congested rail network, limiting its usefulness in its early years.

Plans were drawn up to bypass Bristol with a new line from Wootton Bassett to Patchway and the Severn Tunnel, and to shorten the London to Devon and Cornwall route by linking the Berks and Hants route from Newbury to Westbury and then from Castle Cary to the Bristol and Exeter's Yeovil branch west of Langport. A later three-mile line between Athelny and Cogload was envisaged to speed things further as the initial junction was approached by an extremely sharp curve which trains would have to slow right down for. The 'Great Way Round' tag applied by critics to the Great Western would be removed for good by these two major projects, as well as a third shortening the Birmingham-Bristol route.

In anticipation of these routes, and with growing passenger and freight business stretching the company's locomotive fleet, the Chief Mechanical Engineer William Dean and his (from 1895) Assistant Locomotive Works Manager, George Jackson Churchward, began a series of experiments to assess how best to meet future demand. Some, such as the prototype outside framed 4-6-0

No. 36, proved unsuccessful in traffic, but very quickly Dean and Churchward improved boiler performance by introducing features such as the flat sided Belpaire fireboxes and applied them to the 4-4-0 passenger locomotives being introduced in the late 1890s. This gradual evolution of applying new boilers to proven chassis eventually led to another prototype 4-6-0 which owed little to previous Swindon practice.

No. 100 had outside cylinders, a large Belpaire firebox, a long and wide domeless boiler with few of the graceful curves and flourishes which characterised passenger locomotives of the era. It was at least 25% more powerful than any other passenger locomotive in Britain at the time. It was the last locomotive Dean would have any direct input on, and after he retired in 1902, would provide his successor, Churchward, with valuable clues as to the way forward.

In March 1903, drawing on early experience with No. 100, Churchward put all his ideas developed with Dean into spectacular effect with the introduction of No. 98. Superficially similar to the earlier locomotive, it allied an immensely efficient boiler with outside cylinders and piston valves borne of long experimentation.

It was the prototype 'Saint' and was one of the greatest leaps forward in locomotive design ever. Churchward then took the boiler, cylinders and many other components and built a 2-8-0 locomotive for heavy freight, No. 97, and No. 99, a 2-6-2T which shared the same cylinders but had a smaller boiler and 5ft 8in diameter driving wheels. Within a year Churchward had established a template which would serve the GWR until the very end.

Further designs followed based on standard components – an outside cylinder 4-4-0 designed for passenger duties on routes barred to the big 4-6-0s, a 4-4-2T equivalent, then a 2-8-0T for short-haul heavy freights – with more to come.

1903 saw the Patchway line open, and then three years later, in 1906, the Berks and Hants cut-off was opened throughout. That year also saw the introduction of the 'Cornish Riviera Limited' express - the GWR was blossoming and when the first four-cylinder locomotive emerged from Swindon Works in April 1906 (initially as a 4-4-2 but later rebuilt as a 4-6-0) the company was demonstrably ahead of every other railway in Britain in technical terms. The advent of the GWR's only 'Pacific', No. 111 *The Great Bear*, reinforced this viewpoint but this locomotive was unsuccessful in traffic, and the only real gap in the GWR locomotive fleet was a good general purpose design able to haul passenger and freight traffic alike. This was filled in 1911 with the phenomenally successful '43XX' 2-6-0.

Churchward attempted innovation in coaching stock too. The massive 75ft long 'Dreadnought' coaches only had doors at each end and ditched the fussy clerestory

roofs of the Dean era. Oddly they didn't prove popular with passengers, and although future carriages would retain the elliptical roof, other old traits would continue for decades.

The re-equipment of the GWR was very much a work in progress by the time the First World War broke out – Churchward's standard locomotives were in a minority at the time – but in essence, the GWR of 1914 was recognisably that of the 1930s and even of British Railway's Western Region in the 1950s. The Great War saw the GWR perform prodigious feats and it emerged with its reputation strong. Churchward was awarded a CBE and Collett an OBE in the 1918 Birthday Honours for their service in wartime.

The Grouping Years
It is tempting to suggest that the amalgamations of 1923 which created the 'Big Four' left the Great Western largely untouched – after all, it alone

retained its identity. Nonetheless, the amalgamations with the coal-carrying railways of South Wales, along with the Cambrian Railway, and three narrow gauge lines in the principality (and other English routes too such as the Didcot Newbury and Southampton) inevitably changed the complexion of the company. For one thing, the addition of the coal traffic subtly shifted the company's commercial centre of gravity West, and the Welsh railways had proud and distinguished traditions of their own which complemented the Swindon tradition.

For modellers, however, the focus is invariably on the locomotives. Churchward's final design, the big '47XX' 2-8-0s with 5ft 8½in driving wheels were few in number but regarded as highly useful machines but it was the succession of Collett to the Chief Mechanical Engineer role in 1921 which led to some of the most famous GWR designs of all.

From its early beginnings the GWR produced delightful locomotives, even if its broad gauge was something of an anachronism. GWR broad gauge 4-2-2 *Bulkeley* is seen is as built at Swindon in 1880. Rail Archive Stephenson

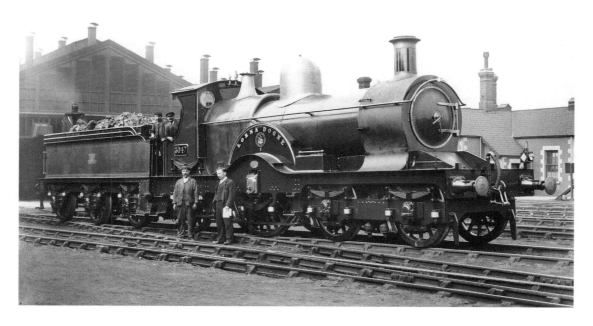

Early GWR locomotives had a flair of design. This is William Dean designed GWR 4-2-2 3047 *Lorna Doone* at Swindon shed in 1900. Rail Archive Stephenson

Swindon Works was the birthplace for thousands of GWR locomotives and later its facilities were utilise by BR culminating in the construction of diesel hydraulics. One of the most modern diesels of the time, 'Western' hydraulic D1047 *Western Lord*, rubs shoulders with '57XX' 0-6-0PT 9666 outside Swindon Works on September 8 1963.
Bob Tuck/Rail Archive Stephenson.

The first was the 'Castle' class of 4-6-0s, led by 4073 *Caerphilly Castle* in August 1923. Collett might well have been better advised to start from scratch rather than enlarging and adapting the design of Churchward's 'Stars' for the new locomotives, but although they were a compromise from the ideal of fitting a '47XX' boiler to a 'Star' chassis on weight grounds, in practice, the 'Castles' were brilliant. Head to head against the London & North Eastern Railway's (LNER's) much bigger 'A1' 'Pacifics' in 1925, the GWR's 4079 *Pendennis Castle* was not only faster and more powerful – it was more efficient too.

So began a locomotive 'arms race' which saw the Southern Railway enter with its 'Lord Nelson' 4-6-0s which were claimed to be more powerful than the 'Castles'. To the brilliant and publicity-minded General Manager, Felix Pole, this was unthinkable and he instructed Collett to prepare a rival design which would eclipse its rivals in tractive effort. After Pole had discovered just four bridges between Paddington and Plymouth needed to be strengthened to accommodate heavier locomotives than

the 'Castles' the game was set and Collett set to work enlarging the 'Star' template to its very limit.

The result was 6000 *King George V*, which was released from Swindon Works in 1927. With a tractive effort of 40,300lbs and a boiler pressure of 250psi, it was as powerful as promised, but in sticking with Churchward practices, Collett had deviated from virtually every standard the GWR had. The wheels were different diameters, the leading bogie cranked from outside to inside bearings to clear the cylinders – and above all the locomotives were so heavy they were limited in where they could run. Despite all these apparent handicaps, the 'Kings' were supremely powerful machines that gave the GWR a relatively small stud of 30 locomotives for the heaviest and most demanding duties of all.

Collett didn't just focus on express designs however. In 1924 he rebuilt a 'Saint', 2925 *Saint Martin*, with 6ft diameter driving wheels as opposed to the 6ft 8½in of the 'Saints' to establish the potential on mixed traffic duties. The prototype proved extremely successful and from 1928 a fleet of follow-ons called

'Halls' spread across much of the GWR system. Another equally successful and even more ubiquitous design appeared in 1929 - the '57XX' 0-6-0PTs. The pannier tanks were a GWR peculiarity – simpler to construct than a saddle tank and with easier access to the inside motion than a side tank. These powerful and punchy little locomotives owed little to Churchward practice, being based on Victorian designs, but they were surprisingly fast and powerful. With 863 built by the GWR and outside contractors, they spread over almost all of the company's system.

And then, from a technical point of view, the GWR's steam locomotive development stagnated by comparison with other railways. Further locomotive designs appeared – the '2251' 0-6-0s and the 'Grange' and 'Manor' 4-6-0s in particular, but by and large the company was content to replicate existing designs in order to maximise the benefits of Churchward's standardisation programme. The company didn't stop innovations though - the Automatic Train Control system was extended over most of the GWR's main lines, and in

The 1930s mark the beginning of what many consider to be a golden age on the railways, and as a spectacle the GWR was unsurpassed. With its bright green locomotives complete with burnished safety valve bonnets and copper capped chimneys hauling chocolate and cream coaches through some of England and Wales' most beautiful scenery, there was little to dislike about the company, and ever since then railway modellers have tried to emulate the grandeur of the company.

However, the GWR wasn't just about glamorous express trains - the coal traffic within and from South Wales was truly epic, and there were constant seasonal flows from agriculture ranging from flowers from the Scilly Isles to Cornish broccoli, Worcestershire plums, cattle from Ireland to Fishguard, and every night trainloads of milk from all over the GWR system. No GWR model would be complete without a significant freight element.

The GWR chose not to follow the London Midland & Scottish (LMS) and London & North Eastern Railways in developing ever more powerful locomotives for prestige services in the

1930s. Instead its focus was on maintaining and increasing its profitability and rightly so because as a public limited company it had a legal duty to do well for its shareholders as well as providing a public service. This focus on making the most of what it had served the country well, particularly in the Second World War, where not only did the GWR play a vital role in keeping people and goods moving; Swindon Works supplied huge amounts of war material and two of the company's paddle steamers even took part in the Dunkirk evacuations of 1940.

Collett retired in 1941, succeeded by Frederick Hawksworth. There was little Hawksworth could do in wartime in terms of new designs, but in his 'Modified Halls' and 'County' 4-6-0s he deviated from hitherto sacrosanct principles by introducing straight plate frames along the whole of their length, abandoning the cylinder and half-saddle construction, and increasing the amount of superheat. The 'Counties', which were introduced from 1945, used a high boiler pressure of 280psi and were intended to approach the 'Castles' for performance, something they never really managed.

The Dean Goods 0-6-0s were one of the great success stories of the pre-Churchward era serving the GWR as well as BR and even assisting in the First World War with the Ministry of Supply. Dean Goods 2426 passes Flax Bourton with an up goods in 1939. Lewis Coles/Rail Archive Stephenson

December 1933 the first of the striking diesel railcars entered service on local services from Paddington. Before long the concept was developed for use on Birmingham to Cardiff expresses which were proving uneconomic to operate with steam traction, and the second batch (which had a higher speed of 80mph compared with the 63mph of Railcar No. 1) performed this role to perfection.

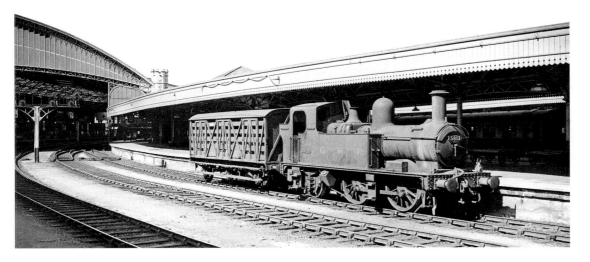

The Collett 0-4-2Ts were best known for their operation with push-pull Autocoaches, but their duties were much more widespread. Still carrying its GWR letters but with a new BR smokebox numberplate, GWR '58XX' 0-4-2T 5813 stands with a milk van at Bristol Temple Meads on June 4 1949. John Wilson/Rail Archive Stephenson.

The GWR ordered a gas turbine locomotive for investigation but before it could be delivered Clement Attlee's Labour government nationalised the railways. The GWR had outlasted all of its contemporaries of 1835 and given us a priceless cultural memory, but from midnight on December 31 1947, it became public property.

The last gasp

At first, nationalisation brought few changes to the former Great Western routes. Other than a slight change of shade on the locomotives to Brunswick Green and to crimson and cream on the coaches it was business as usual. Alone among the 'Big Four', the GWR locomotives retained their original numbers: presumably it was felt too expensive to replace the cast brass numberplates.

Gradually British Railways exerted its authority, with 'Britannia' 4-6-2s gaining currency with their work from Cardiff Canton, and the '9F' 2-10-0s grudgingly held in high regard after teething troubles were ironed out. The problem, as GWR men saw it, though, was that standards were being imposed which were inferior to those they were used to – there was

truth in the old saw that Swindon scrapped components at the tolerances other railways built to.

The final 'Castle', 7037 *Swindon*, was built in August 1950 and these magnificent locomotives held sway throughout the decade. When the regions were allowed some choice in their liveries it surprised nobody that the Western Region opted to paint its coaching stock chocolate and cream once more.

When it came to modernisation, the Great Western's tradition of individuality reasserted itself with a vengeance. Other regions were looking at diesel-electric and electric traction, but the Western Region chose to investigate the possibilities offered by diesel-hydraulic locomotives instead. The decision wasn't about being different for the sake of it, however: the stiff gradients between Newton Abbot and Plymouth meant the diesel-electrics on the drawing board would be no more capable than a 'King'. By contrast the diesel-hydraulics offered a high power to weight ratio, potentially allowing journey accelerations or load increases. The first, the D600 'Warships' proved the concept but compromises made in their construction meant they were heavier than anticipated. The later D800 series

were a purer interpretation of the German designs on which they were based and started to replace 'Castles' and 'Kings', while the D7000 'Hymeks' were intended to supersede the mixed traffic 4-6-0s. The advent of the D1000 'Westerns' from December 1961 finally provided a diesel more capable than the 'Kings' and the rundown of the ex-GWR steam fleet began to gather momentum. The widespread introduction of diesel multiple units descended in concept from the diesel railcars accelerated this process, and the Beeching cuts saw routes and stations closed and services cut. By December 1965 it was virtually all over for Great Western steam, followed shortly after by Birmingham's marvellous Snow Hill station, which reopened in cut-down form in the 1980s.

Thankfully, while the GWR's steam fleet was being withdrawn en masse, railway preservation was starting to blossom and today there are around 30 museums and heritage railways in former GWR territory preserving some aspect of the old company - and that doesn't include other railways which operate ex-GWR locomotives. There is much to see, both on the surviving routes and in preservation: if you travel through the

The GWR pioneered the introduction of diesel railcars in Britain with its fleet of AEC powered single car and two car sets. With a Collett coach sandwiched between railcar W36W leads a special for AEC from Weston-super-Mare into Bristol Temple Meads during June 1953. Eric Fry/ Rail Archive Stephenson.

Capturing the early years of standardisation, GWR '2221' 4-4-2T 2239 leaves Paddington with a semi-fast train for Oxford in 1924. Frank Hebron/ Rail Archive Stephenson.

company's former territory, it is impossible to escape the company's legacy.

Modelling the Great Western

The time is right for a reappraisal of the GWR, particularly for railway modellers. The branch line terminus may seem a cliché but they are eminently attractive from an aesthetic and operating point of view.

The GWR wasn't just about branch lines, however. Modelling the early days from 1838 to the 1860s would pose a lot of challenges as everything would have to be scratch built from the track upwards but a broad gauge layout could offer short train lengths, minimal facilities at stations and locomotive sheds, as well as relatively simple coaches and wagons. Granted, building the locomotives would be a challenge, but in many senses, the first phase of the GWR does make sense for a layout, particularly in a restricted space.

Generally though, modelling the Great Western gets easier as the company develops and as the broad gauge retreats. From 1883, when the 'Dean Goods' was introduced (made by Hornby, but not featured in the current catalogue), it

becomes possible to supplement kit built locomotives and rolling stock with off the shelf products - the 'Achilles' 4-2-2 and '2721' 0-6-0PT are also available from Hornby.

But it is really from Churchward's reign as CME that the number of GWR models increases. Pre-grouping models are still limited however. Bachmann produces good models of the '43XX' 2-6-0 and '45XX' 2-6-2T while Hornby has just produced a new '28XX' 2-8-0 and has offered 'County' 4-4-0s and an incorrectly dimensioned 'Saint' in the past. A decent 'Saint', 'Star' and '5101' would be extremely useful, as would a '4200' 2-8-0T.

Post 1923 models are much more popular, headlined by Hornby's new and extremely good 'Castle'. There are decent models of a wide range of prototypes, including 'Kings', 'Halls', 'Manors', 'Counties' and 'Granges', as well as '57XXs', 2-6-2Ts, '2251' 0-6-0s, 2-6-2Ts and the popular little '48XX' 0-4-2Ts. Predictably there is much less coaching stock and this is a wide open market for the manufacturers: if absolute authenticity is the aim for a pre-1948 layout, it is likely you will have to resort to kits for coaches at least.

The BR period is perhaps the most straightforward of all to model, particularly following the introduction of BR Mk 1 coaches. Most of the principal GWR designs of the post 1955 period are available in decent quality off the shelf form, while there are good models of the 'Hymek', 'Warship' and 'Western' diesels, with the D600s being developed for Kernow Model Rail Centre at the time of writing and Dapol working on an NBL Type 2 (D6300 series) Bo-Bo hydraulic too.

With a little imagination, modelling the GWR doesn't have to involve a rural branch line terminus: what about a suburban station in the industrialised West Midlands or London, or a predominantly freight line in South Wales or perhaps even a section of main line with a small halt? One thing is certain, the GWR offers a feasibly long time frame for a model to be set in and an inexhaustible supply of inspiration.

Read the full story of the GWR

■ Andrew Roden is a well known railway writer and a regular contributor to *Hornby Magazine*. His latest book, *Great Western Railway: A History* is available now, priced £16.99. For more information visit *www.andrewroden.com*

Southern
sunshine

Of all the BR regions, the Southern has received the greatest boost of all through new ready-to-run models in recent years. Showing off the splendour of the smallest of the BR regions, we bring you five of the best Southern layouts to feature in *Hornby Magazine*.

Pimlico, is the result. This atmospheric layout is set in the London suburbs and captures the final years of steam when diesel and electric traction were becoming the norm rather than the exception.

Specifically South Pimlico is based on Colin's memories of his time working in the Lambeth and Southwark areas in the mid-to-late 1970s when he became familiar with the railways of the area. The 1970s period was considered as the theme for the layout, but the 1966/1967 period had a greater appeal and offered the opportunity for a wider range of rolling stock to be operated.

The starting point was an abandoned project bought from a former club colleague, but altered to have a totally urban scene supplemented by suburban passenger and trip freights running in the shadow of typically 1960s buildings and through a cutting edged with stained retaining walls. Even though the layout is his own, Colin is keen to acknowledge the encouragement and advice of his good friends Jim and Charlie Connor of Harford Street fame.

The rationale for the line is that it is presumed to diverge near Clapham Junction and run at a low level via South

Pimlico and then through Kennington and Walworth where it reached ground level and finally to London Bridge. The freight only spur is presumed to run down to a Thames-side coal wharf close to Battersea Power Station.

Track is drawn from Peco's code 75 range with the conductor rail being formed from code 60 rail soldered to the top of brass track pins – an arrangement which has proved to be robust in exhibition life.

Rolling stock is drawn from both kit and ready-to-run sources with Hornby contributing greatly to the steam side of the roster and DC Kits range of EMUs being the main source of multiple units including 2-EPB and 2-HAP units. A Bachmann 4-CEP is also expected to join the fleet in due course. All the stock is at least lightly weathered to give it an in-service look.

Passenger services are worked almost exclusively by 2-EPB, 2-HAP and 2-BIL units, plus there is also an 'unadvertised' steam-hauled passenger working usually hauled by a BR '3MT' 2-6-2T or BR '4MT' 2-6-4T. Freight traffic is usually in the hands of Class 33s and 73s, although a 'Q1' is also regularly used on the layout despite the last being withdrawn in 1966 – modeller's license being the key here.

As a layout South Pimlico conveys the atmosphere of the changing skyline of the late 1960s in the capital and illustrates a period and area which many remember but rarely model.

South Pimlico statistics

Owner:	Colin Whitelock
Scale:	'OO'
Length:	16ft
Width:	18in
Track:	Peco Code 75
Period:	BR Southern Region 1966-1967

Above: A 'Q1' leads a coal train from the main line towards the wharf in the shadow of growing high rise housing. Chris Nevard.

Far left: A kit built BR '3MT' 2-6-2T restarts its van train from a signal check at South Pimlico. Chris Nevard.

Representing the changing face of British Railways in the late 1960s, a pair of 2-HAP EMUs thread between the retaining walls on the approach to South Pimlico. Chris Nevard.

South Pimlico
A visit to Clapham Junction in the 1960s sealed the future for Colin Whitelock's modelling activities and his layout, South

A 'JA' (later Class 73) enters Charlotte Road with an engineer's train while running on diesel power. Mike Wild.

Charlotte Road

Few layouts can compete with the fascinating life that the Wirral Finescale Railway Modellers' Southern Region Charlotte Road has led.

The project was started as a terminus to fiddle yard project in America by Tony Sissons where it featured a 10ft 5in long scenic section and 4ft 5in fiddle yard. This was in 1990, but 20 years later this beautifully modelled 'P4' gauge layout has been a regular part of the exhibition circuit in the UK as one of the foremost Digital Command Control layouts as a continuous run layout!

The layout was invited to ExpoEM2000 in 1999, but at the time it was still in America. Duly it was prepared for the marathon journey across the Atlantic Ocean which saw it fly via Charlotte, North Carolina to Washington DC, then to Amsterdam and finally Manchester. From there it was taken to its new home in North Wales and despite 4,500 miles in transit all that had been affected were a few lumps of coal which had come loose from the coal loading stage!

Once the layout was set up it was decided that it needed completely rewiring, and this was just a few months

before its debut show. Originally it was shown as a terminus to fiddle yard layout, but the crew behind it grew tired of that type of operation and decided to rebuild it as a continuous double track main line. This involved building new scenic boards and a completely new fiddle yard, all of which was accomplished within 12 months ready for the 2004 Warley National Model Railway Exhibition!

Charlotte Road has always been a dynamic layout with continuous changes and the Wirral Finescale Railway Modellers have wholeheartedly embraced digital command control technology for the layout. Digitrax is the system of choice together with computer control of signalling with integrated points and signals and which also randomly generates train movements through a second piece of software.

This layout has now been retired from the exhibition circuit having made its final appearance in October at the Merseyside exhibition in Birkenhead. But that is also the start of a new chapter for the Wirral Finescale Railway Modellers who are already working on their next project.

Charlotte Road statistics	
Owner:	Wirral Finescale Railway Modellers
Scale:	4mm, 18.83mm gauge
Length:	28ft
Width:	10ft
Track:	Scenic section: Point work is a mixture of ply and rivet with C&L cosmetic chairs added plus P4 Track Co kits along with C&L and P4 Track Co plain track. Fiddleyard is copper clad point work with C&L plain track
Period:	1966/1967, BR Southern Region (South West Division)
Featured:	HM36

A London Transport RTL stops to pick up passengers as a BR blue Class 33 moves through Dagnell End with parcels vans. Mike Wild.

Dagnell End

The countryside is often seen as a simpler route in modelling circles as fewer buildings are needed to make a realistic setting. However, for its latest 'OO' layout the Redditch Model Railway Club took a totally different direction by switching to an urban scene set on the Southern Region in the transition era. It even features an Underground section too with London Transport tube trains in operation.

The project developed from the club member's desire to build something different away from the usual rural settings which had become commonplace on their previous layouts. Construction started in February 1998 with the plan of completion within three years. In the end it actually took 11½ years to complete this fascinating South London scenario which replicates the nature of the suburban and main lines which wore their way over and above the streets of London and its outskirts.

Dagnell End is a fictitious suburb of South West London somewhere close to where the real town of Brentford is situated, set in the 1960s. Modeller's licence was used in that the London Underground Piccadilly line to Heathrow Airport is on the surface at

the real location. Some of the buildings in the real location have been used as the basis for the models including the local library and a number of the houses.

Dagnell End is fully wired for digital command control. It is wired on a bus bar principle except that the bar is either a red or black wire. Control is provided by the NCE system after evaluating several options and it has a large control throttle with mainly single shortcut buttons, such as locomotive whistles, when using DCC sound locomotives.

All the buildings on the layout are scratch built and being an urban setting these play an important part in setting the scene. A number of field visits to London gained valuable information on potential buildings for the Dagnell End. In total there are more than 60 buildings, each one scratchbuilt using thick card for the basic structure, although the larger buildings use alternative methods.

Naturally the trains play an important part in placing Dagnell End and a fleet of Electric Multiple Units has been constructed, all scratch built by Ken Bridger and covering 4-TC, 4-EPB, 2-BIL, 2-HAP, 4-BEP, 4-LAV, 4-CIG, 4-BIG, 4-COR and 4-BUF. Beyond this a

fleet of steam and diesel locomotives are also available including 'West Country', 'Battle of Britain' and 'Merchant Navy' 'Pacifics' together with BR 'Standard Four' 2-6-4Ts and other tender locomotives. They run alongside diesel Classes 25, 33, and 47 as well as Class 73 electro-diesels.

Dagnell End statistics

Owner:	Redditch MRC
Scale:	'OO'
Length:	18ft
Width:	11ft
Track:	Peco code 100
Period:	1960s, BR Southern Region
Featured:	HM34

A Drummond 'T9' 4-4-0 waits to depart Chinehurst. Chris Nevard.

Chinehurst

This terminus to fiddle yard layout started out as a test track, but in its 20-year lifespan Chinehurst has been through a series of changes including its track gauge. This shelf layout was started in the early 1990s by Ron North and uses his preferred shelf layout type plan which allows plenty of railway operation to be fitted into the 16ft x 18in floorspace. It currently shares loft space with Ron's American outline 'HO' scale model.

A typical operating session on Chinehurst lasts just over half an hour. Firstly a passenger train arrives and departs. Then the local pick-up freight train arrives and after running round its train proceeds to swap wagons around. This might see the scrap yard mineral wagons arrive empty and depart loaded and the coal wagons arrive loaded and depart empty. Any containers are dealt with at the loading platform either arriving or departing on a flat wagon, vans are merely exchanged with each other at the various sidings.

After the freight train has departed or between operating sessions, the coal loads are removed in favour of scrap loads, these being made on card inserts designed to be easily dropped in or out of the wagons. This sequence is mainly used for home operation as at exhibitions the audience tends to not hang around long enough, or not notice that full coal loads arrive and depart having just delivered them! The layout was originally built to 'EM' gauge using a selection of five good hand built points which Ron had created but had nowhere to use them and this was the raw starting point of the layout we see today.

However, a series of issues including track buckling in the heat and a lack of suitable rolling stock saw Ron convert the layout to 'OO' gauge with Peco code 75 track and with a quick wiring job it was ready for the High Wycombe show in 1998 to replace his under construction North Park. It is now, however, semi-retired in Ron's loft apart from the occasional show visit as a stand-in.

The Southern Region was chosen to reflect rolling stock available in Ron's varied collection, but he also concedes that it might have been better as a Western Region layout as most of his operating crew model that region!

Chinehurst statistics	
Owner:	Ron North
Scale:	4mm/ft 'OO' gauge
Length:	16ft
Width:	18in
Track:	Peco code 75
Period:	British Railways (Southern Region) 1950s–1960s for exhibitions plus the BR blue era at home.
Featured:	HM28

A Billinton 'E4' 0-6-2T enters the yard with goods for shunting. Loaded coal wagons await collection.
Chris Nevard.

A narrow bodied Class 33 moves slowly through Brockley Green with loaded coal wagons from the terminal. Mike Wild.

Brockley Green SE4

Retirement prompted John Wass to build his dream layout and Brockley Green SE4 is the result. Built to 'EM' gauge standards, Brockley Green represents the changing face of BR's Southern Region in South London, with steam, electric and diesel traction all running side by side.

The project started in 2003 when John began planning the layout. The choice of prototype was easy as John has a long history with the Southern. This layout is set on the Nunhead to Lewisham line and it carries a modest rush-hour Electric Multiple Unit (EMU) service as well as steam/diesel goods traffic across London.

Black Cat Baseboards supplied the baseboards, one with two folding legs and the others with just one pair of legs each. They are fixed together with bolts made from lengths of studding iron with a wing nut welded onto one end and a loose one for the other.

The layout's design is very basic, running from a fiddle yard through a half-relief station and on to a second fiddle yard. Both fiddle yards have a six-road traverser mounted onto drawer runners without any pointwork to maximise the space. That concept has probably attracted the most attention at any exhibitions attended so far.

At the time of construction there were several other good Southern electric layouts on the exhibition circuit and to make Brockley Green stand out

John decided to add the overhead wiring system the Southern Region installed in several marshalling yards to negate the use of third-rail there (a real safety risk for shunters of the time).

At the front of the layout a goods yard is connected in both directions directly into the fiddle yards. One road splits at the London or left-hand end, to serve the coal facility and the two tracks at the country end pass through and emerge from the parcels depot. The former has a corrugated iron shed and overhead conveyor system built from Slater's plasticard on a plywood shell and the latter is a Metcalfe cardboard bus garage kit, somewhat modified. The station buildings are based on those at Horsham with its art deco architecture.

The choice of location does allow a good variety of trains to be run – a 4-EPB and a 2-EPB/2-HAP combination of EMUs cover most of the passenger turns while a Class 71 Kent Coast electric locomotive works either a parcels train or a rake of ferry vans. There is also a second train of ferry vans, but these are all 'HO' scale continental examples hauled by a small 'OO' scale locomotive. There are two coal trains – one loaded, one empty – an engineer's train, an oil train and a goods train down via the Widened Lines.

Brockley Green's first outing was in November 2004, only 11 months after being started, at the Hull Model Railway Society exhibition and everything went so well that only slight adjustments were

required. From there it was invited to the prestigious Nottingham show the following March and in September to EXPO EM North. Further exhibition appearances have taken Brockley Green as far as Glasgow, Germany, Belgium and Southwold as well as the NEC for the Warley National Model Railway Exhibition.

By the beginning of 2010 the layout had travelled 6,245 miles to 21 shows averaging 297 miles per show and with more to come.

A Class 71 departs with a trainload of parcels vans. Mike Wild.

A Bulleid 'Q1' working out its final days leads a rake of loaded 21-ton mineral hoppers through the station. Mike Wild.

Brockley Green S.E.4. Statistics	
Owner:	John Wass
Scale:	'EM' (18.2mm gauge, 4mm scale)
Track:	C&L
Length:	13ft 6in
Width:	20in
Period:	BR Southern Region, 1959-1964
Featured:	HM31

Diesel Desires

The past 12 months have witnessed an explosion of new 'OO' gauge diesel and electric model announcements both by the major manufacturers and as exclusive commissions from retailers. **MIKE WILD** analyses the programme and rounds up all of the diesel and electric models due for release in the next two years.

The past 12 months have been the most exciting of all for the 'OO' gauge diesel and electric modeller. Not only have we witnessed a continual procession of new releases covering locomotives as diverse as the BTH Class 15 and Brush prototype HS4000 *Kestrel*, but new announcements have come through thick and fast with more and more retailers stepping up to the mark and commissioning their own ready-to-run models through Bachmann, Dapol and Heljan.

In the past year we've seen Heljan produce models of the BTH Class 15, Clayton Class 17 and Brush prototype HS4000 *Kestrel* which have been joined on the market by delightful multiple units from Bachmann such as a the BR Southern Region 4-CEP EMU and most recently the Cravens Class 105 two-car DMU. Not to be forgotten is Hattons' specially commissioned model of the Class 14 which launched in early 2010.

This, however, is just the tip of the iceberg and one which, for the time being, continues to flourish. Diesel and electric

modelling is at an all time high and in some respects is beginning to over-shadow steam outline models. This is down to the fact that it isn't just the major manufacturers that are planning new models, but retailers too.

Commissioning exclusives

Kernow Model Rail Centre is a leading light in showing the possibilities of commissioning ready-to-run models when it announced the Western Region Class 41 in 2008. This was soon followed by its plans to produce the BR Southern Region Class 205 DEMU in May 2008 and perhaps most spectacularly by its commission to Dapol to manufacture ready-to-run models of the veteran Beattie 2-4-0WTs which operated on the Wadebridge-Wenford Bridge route from 1898 until withdrawal in December 1962. The pace hasn't slowed for KMRC either as on September 4 2010 they also revealed their plans for an LSWR 'O2' 0-4-4T and Southern Region prototype diesels 10201-10203.

Another prolific name in the commission stakes is Hattons of Liverpool. Hot on the heels of the success with its Class 14 commissioned from Heljan, Britain's largest model railway retailer hit the news again in June this year with its plans for a model of the Metrovick Co-Bo in conjunction with Heljan and, just two months later, announcement of exclusive models of LMS prototypes 10000 and 10001 with Dapol.

The story of 10000/10001 in model form is now one of contention for some as two retailers are working on their own independent projects at the same time – the second being Rails of Sheffield. Rails however is working with Bachmann to produce its models and these are expected to be delivered around 12 months after the first of Hattons' models through Dapol.

Also in the news is the iconic Blue Pullman Diesel Electric Multiple Unit (DEMU). DCC specialist Olivia's Trains revealed that it had done a deal with Heljan to produce both the Western and Midland Region power cars with trailer cars becoming available at a later date, but just two months later their plans were shelved as Bachmann revealed it had been working on the same project for nine months previously, but with the intension, at least initially, of only producing the Midland Region six-car set in two liveries.

All is not lost for Olivia's Trains though as at the same time at the Blue Pullman it announced it would be producing the Woodhead EM1 Bo-Bo freight locomotives and EM2 Co-Co passenger electrics in 'OO' gauge. This truly was a revelation for modellers as few could have believed that these two historic designs would ever be turned into ready-to-run models.

Useful websites

■ Bachmann	*www.bachmann.co.uk*
■ Dapol	*www.dapol.co.uk*
■ Hattons 10000/10001	*www.ehattons.com/10000*
■ Hattons Class 28	*www.ehattons.com/class28*
■ Heljan	*www.heljan.dk*
■ Hornby	*www.hornby.com*
■ Kernow Class 41 and 10201-10203	*www.kernowmodelrailcentre.com*
■ Olivia's Trains Class 76/77	*www.oliviastrains.com*
■ Realtrack Models Class 143/144	*www.realtrackmodels.co.uk*

However, as stunning as all this is, there is a potential pitfall – that virtually all of the British diesel and electric locomotives will be available to buy off the shelf within the next two years. Fantastic on one hand, but also limiting the future scope of the market.

There are still classes which haven't been announced as 21st Century models such as the Class 59, Class 67, Class 73, which form part of Hornby's catalogue using ex-Lima toolings with upgraded mechanisms, plus Class 81-84, Class 71 and 74 and a handful of other prototypes which haven't yet been announced.

Multiple option

Of course there are other options away from locomotives and these shouldn't be ignored as there is now a growing market for Diesel and Electric Multiple Units and the range covering both of these subjects is now expanding.

Bachmann has led the way with its third-rail 4-CEP model which is now being followed by a 2-EPB EMU which is due out by the end of 2010. However, beyond this Bachmann is also now working with Kernow Model Rail Centre to produce the 2H Diesel Electric Multiple Unit which opens up another potential avenue for EMUs as

the 2-HAP units consisted of an EPB Motor Brake Second and the same lavatory equipped trailer car paired with the 2H Motor Brake Second while with a little forethought the 2-EPB motor coaches could be used as the basis for a BR 4-EPB. If that wasn't enough the 4-CEP is only one coach and a different set of numbers away from being a 4-BEP buffer equipped unit, but as yet none of these have been announced.

Hornby has also joined the third-rail EMU market by announcing a ready-to-run model of the 4-VEP outer suburban units built in 1967 at York Works. This model is due to be released towards the end of 2010 or the early part of 2011, offering a unit which spanned from 1967, the final year of Southern steam operation, until 2004 when the final slam-door units were withdrawn from general service.

In the DMU stakes Bachmann has again led the way with its Class 108 two-car and three-car units, which have now been followed by two-car versions of the Cravens Class 105. This is to be followed by a model of the Derby Lightweight DMU – the one that started the multiple unit revolution in the 1950s.

Overhead electric modellers are also beginning to get a look in with Bachmann turning its attention to the Class 350 Desiro units which were announced in March 2010.

Let the good times role

It genuinely is the most exciting time for the British diesel and electric modeller. Never before have so many models been available ready-to-run and never before has there been so much to anticipate. What has to happen now is

Hattons and Rails are planning models of LMS prototype diesels 10000 and 10001. 10000 stands at Derby when new on December 12 1947.
Rail Archive Stephenson.

The second third-rail EMU to be produced by Bachmann is the BR 2-EPB. This is the second engineering prototype sample of the model which is now nearing completion.

Bachmann's model of the Freightliner Class 70 is developing rapidly ahead of its planned December/January release date.

that the manufacturers and shops which are taking the commercial risks to make these models possible receive the support of the modellers to keep these dreams becoming reality.

Table 1 lists all the diesel and electric models currently available through Bachmann, Heljan and Hornby, Table 2 (p51) lists the missing links and the following survey rounds up all of the planned diesel locomotive releases and provides an update as to the release date for each one.

English Electric prototypes 10000/10001
Manufacturer: Hattons/Dapol
Manufacturer: Rails/Bachmann
Release date: February 2011/ 2012 respectively
One of the more controversial new commissions is Hattons' announcement of its plans to produce models of LMS prototype diesels 10000 and 10001 in conjunction with Dapol two months after Rails of Sheffield revealed its plans to produce the same pair of pioneer diesels with Bachmann.

However, both projects are going ahead, with Hattons and Dapol planning to release the first of their versions in February 2011, some 12 months ahead of Rails of Sheffield's expected first release. In total 11 variants are planned by Hattons covering all liveries carried by the pair and also weathered versions with Rails planning a similar range.

Bulleid English Electric prototypes 10201-10203
Manufacturer: Kernow/Dapol
Release date: 2012
The most recent of the announcements came on September 4 when Kernow Model Rail Centre revealed that it would be working with Dapol to produce Southern Region diesel prototypes 10201-10203. The model is scheduled for release in 2012 with the major task being creation of the drawings particularly as the detail differences between the first two locomotives (10201-10202) and the third (10203) will be represented. Full details are on Kernow's website and updates will feature in *Hornby Magazine* as the project progresses.

BRCW prototype D0260 *Lion*
Manufacturer: Heljan
Release date: February 2011
Following on from its models of Brush

Table 1 – Ready-to-run diesel and electric models available now

Class	Wheel arrangement	Manufacturer
Class 04	0-6-0	Bachmann
Class 08	0-6-0	Bachmann/Hornby
Class 14	0-6-0	Hattons
Class 15	Bo-Bo	Heljan
Class 17	Bo-Bo	Heljan
Class 20	Bo-Bo	Bachmann/Hornby
Class 24	Bo-Bo	Bachmann
Class 25	Bo-Bo	Bachmann
Class 26	Bo-Bo	Heljan
Class 27	Bo-Bo	Heljan
Class 31	A1A-A1A	Hornby
Class 33	Bo-Bo	Heljan/Hornby
Class 35	Bo-Bo	Heljan
Class 37	Co-Co	Bachmann/Hornby/ViTrains
Class 40	1-Co-Co-1	Bachmann/Hornby
Class 42	Bo-Bo	Bachmann
Class 43 (HST)	Bo-Bo	Hornby
Class 44	1-Co-Co-1	Bachmann
Class 45	1-Co-Co-1	Bachmann
Class 46	1-Co-Co-1	Bachmann
Class 47	Co-Co	Bachmann/Heljan/ViTrains
Class 50	Co-Co	Hornby
Class 52	Co-Co	Heljan
Class 53 (*Falcon*)	Co-Co	Heljan
Class 55	Co-Co	Bachmann
Class 56	Co-Co	Hornby
Class 57	Co-Co	Bachmann
Class 58	Co-Co	Heljan
Class 59	Co-Co	Hornby
Class 60	Co-Co	Hornby
Class 66	Co-Co	Bachmann/Hornby
Class 67	Bo-Bo	Hornby
Class 86	Bo-Bo	Heljan/Hornby
Class 87	Bo-Bo	Hornby
Class 90	Bo-Bo	Hornby
Class 91	Bo-Bo	Hornby
Class 92	Co-Co	Hornby
HS4000 *Kestrel*	Co-Co	Heljan

After several delays Dapol's model of the NBL Class 22 is nearing completion. This is the final artwork for the model which is now in the final stages of tooling work.

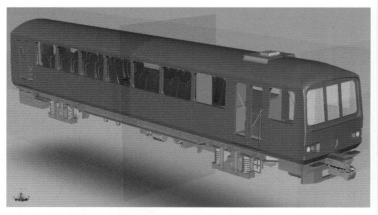

Realtrack Models is working on its Class 143 and 144 models. This is the first **CAD/CAM** artwork to be released indicating the quality of the model.

prototypes D0280 *Falcon* and HS4000 *Kestrel*, it perhaps wasn't a great surprise that Heljan announced its plans to produce BRCW prototype D0260 *Lion* at the Warley National Model Railway Exhibition in November 2009. The model is being tooled from scratch and will be limited to 4,000 pieces. Delivery is anticipated in February 2011 and it will be available solely in the striking white livery of the prototype with five gold strips on the bodyside.

Class 03
Manufacturer: Bachmann
Release date: August/September 2010
Bachmann announced its plans to produce a new model of the Class 03 diesel shunter in February 2009 and the model is now nearing release which was planned during either August or September 2010. The 03 will feature all the hallmarks of Bachmann's latest model including a DCC ready chassis with a 6-pin decoder socket. Three liveries are planned covering plain BR green as D2011 (Cat No. 31-360), BR green with wasp stripes as D2388 (31-361) and BR blue with wasp stripes as 03066 (31-362).

Class 22
Manufacturer: Dapol
Release date: November 2010
Representing Dapol's first venture into 'OO' gauge ready-to-run locomotives is what looks to be a superb model of the NBL Class 22 hydraulics used by the Western Region. The model has been under development for almost two years, but is now nearing completion with the CAD/CAM artwork being cleared for tooling to commence in June this year. The model, which will feature a new five pole super creep motor, is expected to be delivered late this year and hopefully in time for the Warley National Model Railway Exhibition in November.

Class 23
Manufacturer: Heljan
Release date: November 2010
The English Electric Baby Deltic, classified 23, is the subject of Heljan's next major ready-to-run release following on from its work on the Class 15 and 17 during 2008 and 2009. The model was announced in November 2009 and it is expected to be released in November 2010. Heljan is only producing the version with four character headcode panels finished in both BR green with small yellow warning panels and BR blue. Four running numbers will be available – three in green and one in blue.

Class 28
Manufacturer: Hattons/Heljan

Release date: First quarter 2011
Hattons revealed its plan to produce a model of the Metrovick Co-Bo in June this year. The model is being produced for Hattons by Heljan and it is scheduled for release in the first quarter of 2011. In total seven versions are planned covering original BR green, BR green with small yellow warning panels, BR green with full yellow ends and BR blue. Three weathered versions are planned too offering a comprehensive range of models, all with different running numbers.

Class 41
Manufacturer: Kernow/Dapol
Release date: 2011
One of the first models to be commissioned was the NBL D600 series 'Warship' diesel hydraulic which was announced by Kernow Model Rail Centre in March 2008. The model is now nearing the stage where the CAD/CAM artwork is completed and it is scheduled for release during 2011. Five versions are planned covering D600 *Active*, D601 *Ark Royal*, D602 *Bulldog*, D603 *Conquest* and D604 *Cossack*.

Bachmann's Railtrack MPV unit is also making progress, although a final date for its release has not been announced yet.

Heljan is producing the English Electric 'Baby Deltic' in its final form with four character route indicator boxes. On May 10 1966 D9503 departs London King's Cross with empty coaching stock.
Brian Stephenson.

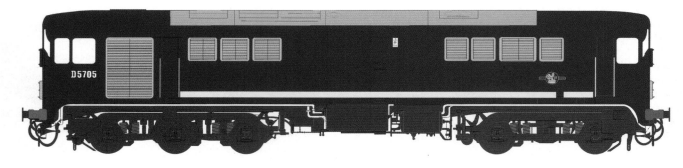

In June Hattons revealed that it was working with Heljan to produce a model of the unique Co-Bo fleet for release in the first quarter of 2011.

The tooling will allow for both original disc headcode and late split headcode versions to be produced including alterations to the grille pattern.

Class 70

Manufacturer: Bachmann
Release date: December 2010/ January 2011

The latest locomotive to enter traffic with Freightliner, the Powerhaul Class 70, is the subject of Bachmann's latest current scene model and two versions are planned for release as 70003 and 70006, both carrying the distinctive Freightliner Powerhaul livery. By July the model had reached the second engineering prototype stage and was about to be approved for production work to begin. The Class 70 is scheduled for release in late 2010 or early 2011.

Class 76

Manufacturer: Olivia's Trains/Heljan
Release date: July 2011

In May Digital Command Control specialist Olivia's Trains wowed electric modellers with its plan to produce ready-to-run models of the Woodhead route EM1 Bo-Bo electric in 'OO'. The model is being produced on behalf of Olivia's Trains by Heljan and both early and late variants are planned. These have a feature laden specification including a 21-pin DCC socket and the option to

Kernow Model Rail Centre's D600 'Warship' model is making progress and the first CAD/CAM drawings are expected soon. In 1958 D601 poses outside Swindon Works between test runs.
Rail Archive Stephenson.

add a sound decoder. Liveries planned for release cover BR black, BR green with small yellow warning panels, BR blue with pre-TOPS numbers and BR blue with TOPS numbers.

Class 77

Manufacturer: Olivia's Trains/Heljan
Release date: TBA

Concurrent with the announcement of the Class 76, Olivia's Trains also revealed that it intends to produce the EM2 Woodhead route Co-Co passenger locomotives. A release date has not been specified for this model yet, but it is expected to follow the Class 76. Three liveries are planned covering original BR black, BR green and BR electric blue. Further details have yet to be advised for this model.

Class 85

Manufacturer: Bachmann
Release date: TBA

Overhead electrics have been in the news this year. In March Bachmann announced that it would be producing the West Coast Main Line based AL5 in 'OO' gauge in original condition and after removal of one of the pantographs. Liveries will cover original electric blue and BR blue, but as yet no official date has been advised for release of the model – it being in the early stages of production.

Derby Lightweight

Manufacturer: Bachmann
Release date: TBA

As a follow up to its models of the Class 105 (see Update on pages 4-5) and Class 108 DMUs Bachmann is also producing a model of the original Derby Lightweight two-car units – the DMUs which started the influx of first generation units. The model is due to be released in BR green, BR green with small yellow warning panels and BR blue, but a release date has not been confirmed.

Blue Pullman

Manufacturer: Bachmann
Release date: TBC

A high profile announcement for Bachmann in July was the revelation that it would be producing the iconic Blue Pullman in 'OO'. The press launch came just two months after Olivia's Trains revealed its plans in conjunction with Heljan, although this project has now been shelved in favour of Bachmann's model. Bachmann announced the Blue Pullman earlier than originally planned and it is expected to take a minimum of 18 months to become available. Only the Midland Pullman will be represented and the unit will be supplied as a full six coach train with a suggested retail price of £300.

Class 143/144

Manufacturer: Realtrack Models
Release date: Third quarter 2011

A new name in ready-to-run 'OO' gauge equipment is Realtrack Models which has revealed its plans to produce models of the Class 143 and 144 Pacer DMUs. The units have a high specification including working directional head and tail lights, a DCC decoder socket, interior fittings and a highly detailed exterior. The Class 144 will be released first and this is expected in the third quarter of 2011 with the Class 143 variant following in 2012.

Class 205 (2H)

Manufacturer: Kernow/Bachmann
Release date: 2011

In May 2008 Kernow Model Rail Centre revealed that it would be working with Dapol to produce a ready-to-run Class 205 Hampshire DEMU for Southern

Region modellers. However, since then the model has been switched to be produced by Bachmann on behalf of Kernow Model Rail Centre to allow it to be prepared for digital sound fitting and also reduce the cost per unit. It is now scheduled for release during 2011 with BR green, blue, blue and grey, Network SouthEast and Connex liveries all being planned.

Class 350 (Desiro)

Manufacturer: Bachmann
Release date: TBA

In a first for overhead electric modellers Bachmann is to produce models of the Class 350 Desiro in 'OO' gauge. The announcement came in March this year and the units will be offered as three-car trains in three liveries of private operators. A release date has yet to be confirmed for this model which is in the course of production.

Class 416 (2-EPB)

Manufacturer: Bachmann
Release date: December 2010/ January 2011

Hot on the heels of the 4-CEP EMU Bachmann is expecting to launch its all new model of the BR 2-EPB EMU in December 2010 or January 2011 offering Southern Region third-rail modellers a second choice of ready-to-run EMU. The model has already been cleared for production following evaluation of the second engineering prototype and it will be available in BR green, BR green with small yellow warning panels and BR blue.

Class 423 (4-VEP)

Manufacturer: Hornby
Release date: Fourth quarter 2010

Joining the fray for Southern Region EMUs, Hornby revealed it is making a model of the BR 4-VEP four-car units in December 2009 and delivery of the model is expected at the end of 2010. The unit will be created in original and refurbished formats and will be available in original BR blue with small yellow warning

panels and Network SouthEast colours. Early samples have already been displayed to the public offering a hint of the quality of this new model.

Waggon und Maschinenbau railbus

Manufacturer: Heljan
Release date: February 2011

In November 2009 Heljan announced that it would be producing models of three of the four-wheel railbuses operated by BR in the late 1950s and early 1960s. The first of these will be the Waggon und Maschinenbau railbus which is scheduled to arrive in February 2011. The model will be available with four different running numbers and a choice of BR green with speed whiskers or BR green with small yellow warning panels. Early indications suggest the retail price will be in the region of £90.

AC Cars Railbus

Manufacturer: Heljan
Release date: TBA

The AC Cars railbus is in the pipeline after Heljan's model of the Waggon und Maschinenbau railbus. At present no date or details have been made public.

Park Royal Railbus

Manufacturer: Heljan
Release date: TBA

Also due from Heljan is the Park Royal railbus, but like the AC Cars version no details or release date have been made public.

Railtrack MPV

Manufacturer: Bachmann
Release date: 2011

Bachmann's model of the Railtrack MPV two-car set has been in the offing for three years now, but at the recent open day the company displayed the first engineering prototype sample of this unusual and attractive model. A release date has yet to be confirmed, but it is expected to be available in shops during 2011.

A high profile announcement has been the revelation that Bachmann is to produce a ready-to-run model of the Midland Blue Pullman. On August 20 1965 the 4.50pm Paddington-Wolverhampton 'Blue Pullman' approaches High Wycombe. Hugh Harman/ Rail Archive Stephenson.

EM1 26014 banks a coal train from Wath past Oxspring Junction signalbox in 1955. Soon scenes like this will be possible in 'OO' with Olivia's Trains commissioned model of the Woodhead EM1. Kenneth Field/Rail Archive Stephenson

Table 2 – The missing diesel and electric locomotive models	
Class	**Wheel arrangement**
BR 'Fell' 10100	2-D-2
English Electric GT3 (gas turbine)	4-6-0
NBL 10800	Bo-Bo
Brown Boveri 18000 (gas turbine)	A1A-A1A
Metropolitan Vickers 18100 (gas turbine)	Co-Co
English Electric DP2	Co-Co
NBL Class 16	Bo-Bo
NBL Class 21/29	Bo-Bo
Brush ES1	Bo-Bo
NER Darlington EB1	Bo-Bo
NER Darlington EE1	2-Co-2
Ashford Class 70	Co-Co
Class 71	Bo-Bo
Class 74	Bo-Bo
Class 80 (Metrovick prototype electric)	A1A-A1A
Class 81	Bo-Bo
Class 82	Bo-Bo
Class 83	Bo-Bo
Class 84	Bo-Bo
Class 89	Co-Co

Kernow's latest diesel commissions are Southern Region prototypes 10201-10203. On August 3 1957 10203 leads the Up 'Royal Scot' near Northchurch tunnel on the West Coast Main Line. C Coles/Rail Archive Stephenson.

Midland magic

The London Midland Region whisked passengers from the great London termini of Euston and St Pancras to the industrial heartlands of the Northwest and onwards to Scotland. Not surprisingly, model railways set on this great network are vast and varied!

A Stanier 'Black Five' thunders past rakes of loaded coal wagons in the exchange sidings at the head of a rake of matching carmine and cream Stanier stock. Chris Nevard.

Braysdown and Writhlington statistics	
Owner:	Alan Parr
Scale:	'EM'
Length:	12ft
Width:	4ft 6in
Track:	Hand built with steel rail
Period:	BR 1950s and 1960s
Featured:	HM27

Braysdown and Writhlington

The Somerset and Dorset Joint Railway network holds a magic and attraction all of its own and for many it is the perfect route to recreate in model form. Its mixture of motive power and wonderful scenery make it highly attractive and this is what drew Alan Parr to the area for this stunning model.

Alan's modelling career started in the 1960s with his passion for Second World War aircraft, but he became tired of the static nature of those creations. In 1970 the railway bug bit when he bought an Airfix Maunsell 'Schools' kit but he didn't know which way to turn

for his railway modelling projects. A visit to Pendon Museum in Oxfordshire provided all the inspiration he needed which lead to the start of this project back in 1975. Between then and 2003 Alan built rolling stock to 'OO' finescale standards, but then a chord struck and he immediately started converting his 15 locomotives, 30 carriages and 150 goods vehicles to 'EM' gauge.

Braysdown and Writhlington captures the spirit of the Somerset & Dorset Railway at the site of Writhlington colliery, which stood just over a mile north of Radstock. The colliery achieved fame in 1973

when it became the last colliery in the Somerset coal field to cease operation, although only faint traces of this once busy and imposing industry remain today.

All the buildings on this layout have been constructed from scratch using plastic sheet and cardboard for the shells with the colliery buildings being overlaid

with DAS modelling clay to recreate the stonework. The signalbox was built by Alan and features full interior detail while the remaining buildings were built by his daughter Carol, some during her exchange in Australia, which were flat packed and sent to the UK for installation. All buildings are lit internally. The working pithead gear was scaled from a photograph and working drawings were created to aid construction.

In terms of rolling stock a broad range of typical BR era Somerset & Dorset stock has been built up for the layout including the erstwhile Fowler '7F' 2-8-0s, 'Black Fives', Bulleid 'Light

Pacifics', Midland '3F' 0-6-0s and more. Within the fleet there is a mix of super detailed proprietary models, brass and whitemetal kits and some scratchbuilt rolling stock Coaches include modified Kitmaster Mk 1s, Comet sides on scratchbuilt or ready-to-run chassis and Ian Kirk kits with freight stock coming from a wider collection of sources.

Before starting Braysdown and Writhlington Alan had never had a desire to build a layout, but thoroughly enjoyed the research, developing new techniques and bringing everything together and by doing so he has created one of the best layouts to be featured in the pages of *Hornby Magazine*.

Viewed from above the colliery an Ivatt '2MT' 2-6-2T ambles past with a stopping train. Chris Nevard.

No model of the Somerset & Dorset Railway would be complete without a Fowler '7F' 2-8-0. 53810 passes Writhlington signalbox with coal empties. Chris Nevard.

A BR '9F' 2-10-0 enters Gas Lane with wagons for the yard. Chris Nevard.

Opposite page: An ex-Lancashire & Yorkshire 'Pug' 0-4-0ST awaits its next call of duty in the sidings. Chris Nevard.

Gas Lane

A request from an exhibition manager spurred the idea for Gas Lane, a layout which measures just 4ft 8½in x 1ft yet offers scope for scenic modelling and operation. Gas Lane has been developed as an addition to Bob's previous layout Condicote (HM7), but was equally designed as a standalone project.

For the basis Bob turned to a gas works which has created a shunting puzzle style layout based, in the main, around the superb cast resin gas works buildings produced by Hornby. Researching gas works proved to be something of a challenge as little information has been recorded about these sites. However, having discovered Fakenham Gas Works – England's only surviving complete gas

works – Bob had a starting point and began by visiting the site to view the buildings and layout of the site.

Not wanting to be tied down to a particular era or period, Bob developed the layout so that it could represent any period between 1910 and 1970 by adding or removing a few specific details which would date or place the layout.

One of the keys to Gas Lane is its

apparent illusion of space. This has been achieved by carefully aligning the buildings and dividing the layout into three zones: the grimy industrial gas plant, the damp and overgrown headshunt and, in between these, the well tended gardens of the manager's house.

It is the details of Gas Lane which really bring it to life and this is where

Gas Lane statistics	
Owner:	Bob Vaughan
Scale:	'OO' (4mm:1ft)
Length:	4ft 8½in
Width:	1ft
Track:	Peco code 75
Era:	1910-1970
Featured:	HM29

research came into play again together with modellers intuition. Look into the neat garden of the manager's house and you'll see a tri-cycle, flower beds, benches and even a lawn roller. Around the railway there are various cameos created by careful selection and positioning of suitable people which all add life and character to the scene.

As a layout Gas Lane is a wonderful creation and one which oozes atmosphere while also offering a compact space to enjoy the fine quality of modern model mechanisms. Perhaps it may be too small for some, but in our eyes its character is what makes its charm and Bob is the first to admit that an exhibition weekend passes quickly when shunting the yard.

A Fowler '4F' 0-6-0 enters New Haden Colliery with empty wagons for loading. **Mike Wild.**

At the colliery screens an Andrew Barclay 0-4-0ST propels wagons for loading. Mike Wild.

New Haden Colliery

The industrial landscape of a colliery setting can make a wonderful basis for a model railway, not least because of the intensive operation that this type of industry requires. A little over 20 years ago the Stafford Railway Circle started building New Haden Colliery – one of the collieries on the Cheadle branch in Staffordshire.

A new book by Allen Baker inspired the layout and it serves as a model of a small part of the Cheadle branch which was just over four miles long and joined the North Staffordshire Railway Stoke-Derby line at Cresswell. The colliery at

New Haden was one of the primary reasons for the line and engineers had to tunnel through a hill at Draycott Cross for the railway to reach the colliery. As well as coal traffic the line saw passenger services, pick-up goods and, in its final

years, sand with the whole line being operated on a one engine in steam basis – this meant that at Cresswell the driver would collect the staff from the signalbox unlocking the points to the branch and that no further trains would be allowed

New Haden Colliery statistics	
Owner:	Stafford Railway Circle
Scale:	'EM'
Length:	22ft 6in
Width:	3ft 6in
Track:	Hand built
Period:	BR 1950s-1960s
Featured:	HM32

onto the branch until the train returned to Cresswell with the staff.

Originally the layout was referred to as Huntley Cross Colliery derived from two local villages but this was later changed to New Haden Colliery once construction commenced. Having decided to model the location accurately, the Stafford Railway Circle members set about a detailed research programme to develop the buildings, structures and railway layout. This was difficult as few people photographed collieries in the 1940s, but perseverance paid off as the club was lucky enough to acquire plans of the colliery in its later years.

New Haden runs in the 1950s and early 1960s period even though the mine had by then closed together with the tunnel. Rather than choose 'OO' gauge for the track, 'EM' gauge was selected by the group meaning that locomotives have been built from kits to suit this scale together with re-gauged wagons and carriages to operate the layout.

Trains of empty wagons arrive at the yard and are shunted around the colliery by industrial locomotives before being despatched as loaded workings onto the main line again. This apparently simple practise is made all

the more realistic by loose coal being loaded through the colliery screens into the wagons meaning that the operators are always kept busy when the layout is on show.

New Haden has seen a number of improvements behind the scenes during its life on the exhibition circuit and even now there are still plans to improve the removal of loose coal from the wagons once the trains reach the off-scene fiddle yard. It continues to be a popular layout on the exhibition circuit and more information can be found at *www.staffordrailwaycircle.org.uk* or in HM32.

Fairburn 2-6-4T 42234 crosses the road to the south of New Haden Colliery with the passenger service. Mike Wild.

A 'Princess Royal' 4-6-2 thunders along the lower main line with a Travelling Post Office working as a Fairburn 2-6-4T approaches the station on the upper level. Trevor Jones.

Dalby Wood

Dalby Wood is the latest layout to be built by the 'OO' gauge section of the Warley Model Railway Club. Growing on experience with their previous layout, Halston Junction, the group has aimed to develop an interesting and exciting slice of railway operation which has been lifted further by the double level nature of the railway.

The upper and lower levels are independent of each other and each level has its own hidden storage area to the rear of the layout. The upper level pre-dominately operates with BR London Midland and Western Region motive power while the lower level concentrates on the Eastern Region with a handful of Midland trains too.

The range of locomotives and rolling stock available for this layout is immense. In total there is a stud of more than 200 locomotives available – 80 being required for an exhibition – plus more than 150 carriages and 160 goods vehicles. All this adds up to a busy and fulfilling layout which keeps both the public and the operators equally enthralled. Add to this steam locomotives fitted with smoke units and you start to see the potential of this 21ft x 16ft monster. There also some unique models within the collection including models of the Blue Pullman Diesel Electric Multiple Unit and English Electric gas turbine GT3 making it well worth watching this layout for sometime at a show.

The layout made its public debut at the Warley National Model Railway Exhibition in November 2009 and has a series of bookings for exhibitions until 2012 already. Construction has been carried out over a number of years and the layout features SMP flexible track to 'OO' gauge, but with correct sleeper spacing, plus hand built points. As well as creating appropriate train formations the Warley club members have also installed working colour light signals which combined with infra-red detectors allow signals to reset to red after the passing of a train.

The lower level is simple in its layout featuring a double track main line with a goods loop on each circuit. The upper level however is more complex as it features a station and goods yard as well as a range of suitable industrial and residential buildings which complete the picture.

Dalby Wood is a true exhibition layout and it only attends three shows per year which allows the team behind it to continue to develop and detail it. For the full feature on Dalby Wood see HM41 and it can also be seen in action on Hornby Magazine DVD No. 1.

Dalby Wood statistics	
Owner:	Warley Model Railway Club
Scale:	'OO'
Length:	21ft 6in
Width:	16ft
Track:	SMP with hand built points
Period:	BR 1950s/1960s Midland and Eastern Regions
Featured:	HM41

Gas turbine prototype GT3 leads an express on the upper level as a BR 'Britannia' crosses paths with a '4F' on the low level. Trevor Jones.

At the station a 'Black Five' approaches the busy platforms while an 04 diesel shunter works the yard. Trevor Jones.

A BR Sulzer Type 2 draws steel plate wagons through the yard at Dalry Road. Mike Wild.

A Class 08 takes charge in the industrial sidings delivering wagons to factories. Mike Wild.

A Clayton Type 1 leads trestle wagons out of the factories for onward movement. Mike Wild.

Dalry Road

The five year period from 1965-1970 is rarely modelled, but Ian Atkinson bucked the trend with his delightful 'O' gauge freight layout which is firmly sited in this period in central Edinburgh.

The Scottish Region of the time was almost exclusively diesel operated and Ian has been able to take advantage of the variety of colour schemes to be seen at the time by covering BR green with small yellow warning panels, BR green with full yellow ends, early BR blue schemes and more.

Dalry Road is set in central Edinburgh and focuses on a goods yard which was situated around one mile from Princes Street and just next to, but above, Haymarket station. The layout features a small locomotive depot, arrival and departure roads, coal drops, industrial sidings and more. The whole 24ft x 4ft layout is scenic with a small hidden fiddle yard neatly tucked behind industrial buildings to one end. This has allowed the maximum potential for scenic modelling to be drawn from the layout's footprint and maintain the greatest area possible for railway operations.

In operation Dalry Road is fairly straightforward in concept. From the fiddle yard trains head into the arrivals/departure sidings where a diesel shunter (usually a Class 08) couples to the train and hauls it into the goods yard, releasing the train engine. The train engine then moves to the depot while the shunter takes the wagons where they're needed. Then the operation is reversed, with the train engine moving onto the departing train to release the shunter for the next move.

It sounds and is deceptively simple, but add the need to shunt the locomotive depot, shunt the wagons to the correct sidings and not get everything tangled up and Dalry Road becomes a very interesting shunting layout with some intensive operation. Control is analogue with two controllers – one operates the yard and the other the opposite end of the layout – but each can operate the whole layout if needed. It's a reasonably simple method which works well.

However, Ian didn't build Dalry Road – he bought it. Since becoming its proud owner, he has added scenery here and there including grown trees from Rural Railways, more vehicles, cars, trucks, vans, fork trucks and people from lots of different sources. Most of these have been painted by Roger Whittam who was the wargaming world champion in 2010.

Locomotive power is provided for by three Class 08 shunters (one DA Model engineering kit and two Brassworks/ Tower Models products) with two in green and one blue. There is also a pair of Class 17 'Clayton' Bo-Bos – D8586/87 which were the only two fitted with Rolls-Royce engines – and a pair of Tower Models Class 20s.

One of the Class 20s was bought from Dave at Tower Models which turned out to be a Scottish one with tablet catcher equipment, while the other was acquired from a modeller in Yorkshire only to discover when it arrived that they were consecutive numbers and both had the tablet equipment. There is also a Class 24 in BR green, a Class 25/1 in green, a Class 25/3 in blue, and a Class 26 and Class 27 in green. Wagons are built from ABS, Connoisseur, Freight Man, Peco, Parkside Dundas, and Slater's kits. Most of the stock is weathered to varying degrees to provide as realistic a scene as possible.

One of the benefits of Dalry Road is that most of the stock can be seen on the layout most of the time, as rolling stock only changes in the fiddle yard. The challenges of operation are great and its scenery befitting of the urban area in which the real Dalry Road is located.

Dalry Road statistics	
Owner:	Ian Atkinson
Scale:	'O'
Length:	24ft
Width:	3ft
Track:	C&L Finescale
Period:	BR 1965-1970, Scottish Region
Featured:	HM36

Making a start in
locomotive
detailing

Today's ready-to-run locomotives come with impressive amounts of detail as standard. However, adding supplied components is not always easy and there is always room for some further improvements. **JAMES LAVERY** shares some tips on how to enhance your traction fleet.

With the great strides made by the likes of Hornby, Bachmann and Heljan over the past decade, it is sometimes thought that there's nothing to be added to most ready-to-run (RTR) locomotives. There have also been debates about how modellers have been losing the impetus to undertake 'real modelling' tasks.

While there are some truths in these statements, there are also some myths. For example, even the highest specification 'OO' gauge locomotives of recent years can still be improved with a few extra components fixed in place and, besides, is it so bad to be able to leave behind the need for remedial work on our new purchases and to concentrate on the actual building and operation of our layouts?

The days of accepting compromises from manufacturers have gone, with the constant raising of the bar from each manufacturer in turn maintaining a healthy competition and providing consumers with

What we used	
Comet	
LS35 BR Standard pattern footsteps	£2.75
Springside	
Fire irons set for tank locomotives	£3.25
Fire iron set for tender locomotives	£3.25
LNER head lamps	£3.25
GWR head lamps	£3.25
Mainly Trains	
MT355 chequer plate	£1.45
MT316 smokebox door handle	£1.60
MT356 coupling hooks	£1.45
MT187 lamp brackets	£3.50
MT256 Loco details, including cab doors	£2.40

Suppliers

Comet Models,
105 Mossfield Road, Kings Heath, Birmingham B14 7JE
Tel: 0121 242 1740
Website: *www.cometmodels.co.uk*

Mainly Trains,
Unit C, South Road Workshops, Watchet TA23 0HF
Tel: 01984 634543
Website: *www.mainlytrains.co.uk*

Springside Models,
2 Springside Cottages, Dornafield, Ipplepen TQ12 5SJ
Tel: 01803 813749
Website: *www.springsidemodels.com*

Aidan Campbell figures,
22 Queens Road, Hoylake CH47 2AH
Website: *www.aidan-campbell.co.uk*

Fox Transfers,
4 Hill Lane Close, Markfield Industrial Estate, Markfield LE67 9PN
Tel: 01530 242801
Website: *www.fox-transfers.co.uk*

Gaugemaster (suppliers of Deluxe Materials glues),
Gaugemaster House,
Ford Road, Arundel BN18 0BN
Tel: 01903 884321
Website: *www.gaugemaster.com*

both more choice and higher quality products. Anyone of a certain age will remember how some brands (mentioning no names!) would routinely offer locomotives in dubious livery shades, with wildly inaccurate detail fittings, heavily recessed glazing and enormous tension lock couplings added to each end. These days, however, it may only be the need to add a footplate crew, plus some coal in the tender that will produce a truly authentic scale model.

What is there to do?
Due to limitations in production processes, problems with delicate parts coming adrift during shipping and the realisation that some users prefer the omission of certain 'extras', many new locomotives are supplied with small (or large) bags of detailing parts to be added by the consumer. The volume of parts varies widely according to prototype and manufacturer, as does the ease with which they can be fitted.

One example is the ViTrains range of Class 37 and Class 47 diesels which require a large number of parts to be cut from plastic sprues and fixed in position – this has the advantage of saving on production costs and maintaining a lower retail price for customers. However, adding these items is not a quick and

simple task, raising the issue of whether these products are truly ready-to-run or semi-finished models. This is down to personal choice. Some like the way models come from the box, whereas others won't accept any compromises.

Whatever your preference, it doesn't hurt to possess a few basic modelling skills (and a small toolkit) in order to make such tasks easier. Gaining experience and confidence in these areas also opens up the potential for other projects to be undertaken, making use of older or budget range models, for instance, bringing them up to a similar specification to more modern ready-to-run offerings.

There's a huge range of after-sales components on the market, for a staggering array of potential detailing or conversion projects, some sources being listed in the accompanying Suppliers panel. The choice of how far to go, in terms of what extra details to add, is entirely up to the individual and it's surprising how much different a model can appear with just a few tweaks here and there.

The projects illustrated here are quite restrained compared to some of the possibilities available, but they show how a few simple techniques can be harnessed to add missing details or improve existing aspects of a model, as well as fitting crucial items such as crew, lamps and coal loads.

While this Bachmann Class 24 comes complete with detailing accessories, picking out the various bufferbeam hose connections in the correct colours completes the job.

Glues

Cyanoacrylate, or 'superglue', is one of the most useful adhesives to locomotive detailers as it will stick virtually anything to anything. However, it has its limitations and can also react unfavourably with clear plastic or painted surfaces, leaving a white, cloudy appearance. Odourless formulas are available to avoid such problems and should be used in proximity to any glazing.

Only small amounts of cyano-type glues should be used for each task and it is always better to decant a small blob onto a scrap of card and then to apply the desired amount to the component using a sharpened matchstick or cocktail stick. This will avoid excess glue from being squeezed out from joints, which will be very hard to remove once set.

Epoxy glue is perfect for adding new parts that are quite bulky, such as metal

buffers, footplate crews or brass coupling hooks. It can be a messy medium, although it can be cleaned up with a damp cloth before it cures and different brands offer a variety of working times, from 5 to 20 minutes, before the joint becomes permanent.

For plastic-to-plastic joints, liquid poly cement can be the best solution as these chemicals work to 'weld' the parts together. When adding coal chippings to a steam locomotive, PVA-based glues are perfect as these will also adhere well to the plastic of the model.

Detailer's Toolbox

Only a handful of tools is required for the lion's share of detailing tasks, the essential items consisting of: scalpel with a supply of fresh blades; tweezers; fine pliers; miniature screwdrivers; needle files; mini drill and bits; rubber cutting mat; steel rule. A supply of fine abrasives, such as wet/dry paper (240, 360, 600 and 1,000grit), suitable adhesives and modelling paints (to touch in the new parts) are also required.

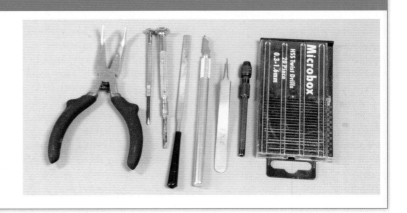

The basic skills of a locomotive detailer include trimming, drilling, handling small parts and being able to achieve neat glue joints. The following steps introduce each of these techniques.

1 Many of today's 'OO' gauge models come supplied with a variety of components intended for fitting by the customer. This Bachmann Class 24 is provided with a full complement of bufferbeam hoses, handrails and disc headcodes.

2 In many cases, the parts can be fitted without dismantling the model. However, drivers are seldom fitted or, if they are, only one is provided at the 'No.1' end. Prior to the 1980s, trains were often double-manned, so adding further staff is important. Use epoxy glue to secure the figures, trimming them to fit into the seats if necessary. Leave to set overnight before refitting, so as not to trap any harmful fumes inside the bodyshell.

3 Painting the interiors also helps, picking out dials, controls, instruments and various conduits where appropriate, as has been done to this Bachmann Class 08. Try and find prototype images to discover the correct colours to use.

4 When fitting detailing parts, never apply glue directly from the jar. Instead, decant onto some scrap card or plastic and use a cocktail stick to dab just a tiny drop of adhesive where it is needed. Handle parts with tweezers or fine pliers.

5 Invariably, mounting holes may be too small for the parts in question, having become clogged with paint during manufacture. Choose a drill bit fractionally larger than the mounting lug of the component and open out the respective hole on the locomotive.

6 Other parts, such as these steam heat pipes, feature square-section lugs. Opening out a square hole is not so easy, so try trimming the lug with a sharp knife until a good fit is achieved. Watch those fingers though!

7 Always undertake a 'dry-run' without glue to ensure a good fit. Allow just a little slack in the joint to leave room for the adhesive, otherwise the glue will squeeze out when the component is pressed home.

8 Other parts, such as these headcode discs, may benefit from the tidying up of moulding 'flash' (excess material) and from drilling-out of the aspect holes. This is particularly important if, like this model, working lights are fitted.

Far left: This budget Hornby model makes a cost effective alternative to the more refined Bachmann '9F', even with the added cost of detailing parts.

Left: A footplate crew, shovel and cab doors enhance the cab of the '9F'. Picking out the various copper pipes and brass valves with paint brings out the existing detail.

New lamp brackets, smokebox door handle, couplings and oil lamps enhance this Bachmann '57XX'.

HOW TO DO IT Going a little further

By using the same techniques, while also adding a few extra strings to your bow, some slightly more adventurous projects can be attempted. Working on models, although still in the current ranges of Hornby and Bachmann, that are of a slightly older 'vintage', they can be brought up to current standards by adding a few small parts.

Cutting away existing parts can seem rather daunting, especially after spending your hard earned cash on a model! But fear not, working slowly and patiently and with the right tools, adding improved buffers, smokebox door handles and lamp brackets can be achieved in just a few hours' work.

1 This Bachmann LNER 'J72' 0-6-0T owes its origins to a Mainline product from the 1970s and, as a result, the moulds are now showing signs of age. Pronounced seams along the boiler and chimney spoil the 'front-end' looks, but can be removed with abrasive paper. Use successively finer grades until the seam has gone and the surface is smooth, working to maintain the boiler and chimney's profile.

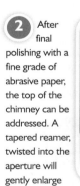

2 After final polishing with a fine grade of abrasive paper, the top of the chimney can be addressed. A tapered reamer, twisted into the aperture will gently enlarge the hole. Work slowly, checking that enough material is retained so as not to weaken the plastic moulding.

3 If the chimney is moulded as a solid unit, such as fitted to this Hornby Railroad '9F', drilling-out the holes makes a big visual impact. Use a hand-held pin vice (not a power drill!) and start with a small diameter bit (1.5mm), working in 0.25mm increments up to around 3.5mm. Working gradually in this way reduces the risk of damage.

4 The 'face' of a steam locomotive is very important and enhancing features on the front of the smokebox can bring great benefits. Older models often sport over-sized moulded door handles that are best replaced. Carefully cut away the plastic, a little at a time until nearly flush. Finish with abrasive paper, again working through the grades until the surface is smooth and flat.

5 Buffers can be treated in the same way, having pulled away any metal heads that are push-fitted into plastic shanks. It can sometimes be tricky not to disturb surrounding rivet detail, but using a knife blade in a scraping action makes it easier to control the tool whilst removing the last of the unwanted plastic.

6 Cast or turned metal replacement buffers are freely available and simply require a mounting hole drilled and the parts fixed in place. Either epoxy or a strong cyano-type glue may be used, ensuring that the new parts are sitting straight and level before it sets hard.

7 Replacement smokebox door handles come in various forms, but this kit, from Mainly Trains, consists of a base and two handles that are threaded onto the boss. Mark and drill a mounting hole for the base, add the two handles and fix them in place with a dab of cyano glue.

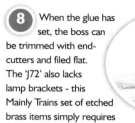

8 When the glue has set, the boss can be trimmed with end-cutters and filed flat. The 'J72' also lacks lamp brackets - this Mainly Trains set of etched brass items simply requires cutting from the fret (with a knife on a scrap of plywood) and folding to shape with pliers.

9 The Mainly Trains pack provides various patterns of lamp bracket, including Western Region style units that are perfect for this particular '9F'. Etched brass chequer plate, cut to shape, makes up the distinctive steps on the buffer shanks and smokebox access step. Fix small details like these in place with just a dab of cyano glue.

10 Another facet of the Railroad '9F' that can be improved is the front pony truck. Use a junior hacksaw to cut away the footsteps from the metal casting and a flat file to tidy the face of the component. Thoroughly clean the unit of metal filings and re-lubricate the axle before re-fitting to the chassis.

11 Etched footsteps are to be fitted to the locomotive's running plate, as per the prototype. These parts, from Comet, must be folded to shape, with the edges of each step curled up a little. The middle step also needs gluing into a slot provided. Allow to set completely before fitting to the engine.

12 On this '9F', the mounting bracket of the footsteps must be cut away (heavy duty scissors will do) and the parts fixed to the casting behind the bufferbeam. Cylinder drain pipes, fitted into pre-drilled holes, have been formed from jeweller's copper wire (from Hobbycraft stores) and glued in place.

13 Overlaying printed name and numberplates with etched versions adds realistic relief to the sides of locomotives. Check that none of the original legend will show behind the replacement first! Smear the smallest blob of cyano to the rear of the 'plate and carefully place in position. This GWR numberplate is from the Fox Transfers range (see Suppliers panel).

14 Real coal chippings in a tender or bunker cannot be beaten for realism and it's a simple matter of brushing some PVA glue over the moulded version and sprinkling on some more authentic material!

15 Another area where the '9F' can be improved is in replacing the cab glazing. This can be pushed out with a small screwdriver and a liquid glazing medium added. A small bead of Glue 'n' Glaze has been run around all sides of each aperture before a clean cocktail stick is used to draw the liquid film across. Leave overnight to set, after which the material will be crystal clear.

16 Along with footplate crew (fixed with epoxy glue), a final touch is to add a set of oil lamps. No steam locomotive would have run without the correct lamp code displayed, even in daylight. Tacky Wax is a temporary adhesive that leaves no residue, allowing the lamps to be repositioned at will.

Country bus depot

As Britain's railways began to suffer increased competition from road transport, depots began to spring up around the country to service the growing fleets of motor buses. **JAMES LAVERY** describes building a typical local facility for a 1960s period scene.

All forms of road transport grew in importance between the two World Wars, helped in part by the wholesale road improvement programmes of the time. Not only did the volume of cars and lorries increase dramatically, but so too did the number of buses. While being previously confined to operating within cities and larger towns, buses soon began to serve smaller, outlying districts with more frequency. Such services were eventually

Located adjacent to the local railway station, Waytown bus depot is perfectly sited to capture passengers from the trains.

cited by BR as justification for closing countless rural branch lines.

As immortalised in the Ealing film *The Titfield Thunderbolt*, the idea of buses replacing railways could be an emotive one. However, it is a fact of history and something that ought to be recreated in miniature.

Moreover, many layouts, even those set in the most rural of locations, would benefit from the inclusion of some form of bus stop, shelter or even a local depot.

Bus stations and interchanges were also common in small towns, particularly from the 1960s onwards, often linking railway stations with the heart of the neighbouring villages or towns – not least as many rail routes passed some distance from the settlements that lent their name to the stations.

The Premise
Waytown, the Scenes from Life layout, has been under construction for the past two years and features every month in

the pages of *Hornby Magazine*. From its inception, a bus depot was deemed an essential feature for inclusion on the layout, depicting as it does a small town somewhere in the heart of England in the early to mid 1960s. This was the time of major impact upon the branch lines of Britain and, as was often the case, the bus depot has sprung up on land directly adjacent to Waytown station.

The railway is in a precarious position, the line already having closed as a through route and the presence of the bus depot must be heightening the fears of complete closure. During the previous large-scale culling of surplus railway routes in the mid-1930s, Waytown lost some of its extensive goods sidings and the land has since been given over to allotments, a scrap dealer and a new housing development. The 1930s also saw a small depot built to accommodate a fleet of motor buses belonging to the Albert Stubbins Transport Company, who began operating services to the larger of the outlying villages, providing a cheap and regular service into Waytown, for the markets and the chance to travel further afield by rail.

However, the railway maintained the upper hand for the ensuing three decades, taking a much more direct route to the nearest important locations; the narrow country lanes are forced to wind their

way over or around the surrounding hills. The local roads have been little improved since they were first metalled in the late 1920s and the buses and lorries are finding it harder to navigate their way through the agricultural landscape.

As the 1960s draw on, there are moves to build new roads and widen existing routes as part of the plan to increase the population of Waytown,

with new housing already under construction. Coupled with the contracting rail network, will this give the bus operators a definite advantage?

Building the scene

At the heart of this scene is an aged but attractive plastic kit offered, until recently, in the Dapol 'OO' gauge range. Having once been produced way back in the real

Virtually all bus depots would boast a tow truck on site, in case of a breakdown. The yard also houses an array of spare parts, including the odd engine, all formed from spare parts from various vehicle kits.

STUBBINS TRANSPORT - WAYTOWN DEPOT

Producing your own sign to replicate a specific real or imaginary bus company is simple enough using any home computer and a colour printer.

1960s by Airfix, the moulds are obviously not as clean as they once were, leaving the modeller to remove areas of waste plastic before construction can begin. Although no longer in the current range, examples of this kit can still be found in model shops, at swapmeets or via second-hand model dealers.

Boasting typical 1930s Art Deco styling, in common with other ex-Airfix products within this range, the kit is redolent of many Interwar depots that sprang up all over the British Isles, at a time when bus operators were in the ascendancy.

Other similar options for 'OO' gauge include a very similar structure in 'ready-to-plant' form from Hornby Skaledale, while Bachmann Scenecraft also has a very attractive structure in its range, albeit of a much larger depot. Metcalfe produces a card kit of a Bus Garage in both 'N' and 'OO', again of 1930s style but of a larger, three gabled shed with folding doors and a separate two-storey administration block. This would be a perfect installation for a large town or city location (see www.metcalfemodels.com). Superquick boasts an attractive 'OO' gauge card kit in its range (ref.B34) which can also be used as a 1930s aircraft hangar.

Aside from the infrastructure, there is a vast range of 'OO' gauge buses to choose from, across the eras, from Oxford Diecast, EFE, Britbus, Corgi and other manufacturers. The choice for modellers in 'N' is currently fairly small, but is steadily growing with Oxford Diecast offering a growing range of out of the box items and Bachmann on the verge of launching its own range of 'N' gauge buses. There are plenty of kits available in both scales too should you want something a little out of the ordinary.

In contrast to the modern scene, where a handful of national firms hold something of a monopoly over bus services, the pre-1980s era saw plenty of local bus companies, either as private or family firms, with a variety of colour schemes.

Alternatively, local corporations also ran bus services, offered as a public service rather than purely profit-driven concerns.

What we used:

Dapol
- ■ Country Bus Depot kit, approx £9.00

Evergreen Plastic
- ■ Pack 143 1.5 x 1.0mm strip £2.65

Dart Castings
- ■ MSV57 Bus Crew £2.40

Harburn Hamlet
- ■ SS387 Petrol pump (pack of 3 with base) £12.21
- ■ FL150 Oil drums £4.59

Langley Models
- ■ F21 Country Bus shelter and bus stop £6.00

Mainly Trains
- ■ MT266 Etched spear fencing £2.85

Britbus
- ■ L004 Leyland Titan PD2 Beadle, Southdown £18.00

EFE
- ■ 26805 Leyland Duple half-cab, Ribble £15.00

Corgi Trackside
- ■ DG114007 AEC Wrecker, BRS £9.00

1 Although dating back over four decades to Airfix days, the Dapol bus depot kit can still be obtained and can be built into an attractive and realistic model. As well as the main walls and roof, separate windows and drain pipes are provided, along with a range of self adhesive signs.

2 Assembly is simple, with the four walls fitting together well. Check that the corners are square using a setsquare and make use of Poly Cement adhesive to create strong, neat joints. Masking tape makes for a useful clamp while glue sets.

3 Due to the age of the kit's moulds, there may be some imperfections in the surface or gaps at the corners. Plastic model filler, such as Revell Plasto, can be smeared over the affected area and left overnight to harden.

4 Abrasive paper, such as 400grit wet/dry paper, is perfect for rubbing down filler once it has set. Flatten the areas in question and then move to finer grits (600-1,000) to remove any scratches and to leave a smooth, even finish.

5 The long rectangular apertures on the ground floor may not be entirely realistic, so adding strips of plastic to form vertical supports may be a good idea. Evergreen plastic strip (1.5 x 1.0mm) has been used here, fixed with Poly cement at equally spaced intervals.

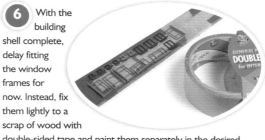

6 With the building shell complete, delay fitting the window frames for now. Instead, fix them lightly to a scrap of wood with double-sided tape and paint them separately in the desired colour. When the building is finished, they can be added to give a neater finish.

An independent fuel supply for the fleet of buses was a common feature of country bus depots.

Bus depots could be hazardous environments so passengers would board at an external stage, a shelter being provided for comfort. This small shelter and stop sign is from Langley Models.

Within the available model ranges, there is considerable choice of region and livery although fictional or more obscure operators may have to be created by repainting or rebranding proprietary buses. If you are striving for realism a little research into bus operators in the area of your intended model will be worthwhile.

Integrated transport?

In the fictional world of Waytown, the local corporation follows a uniquely enlightened approach to integrated transport, working in the knowledge that if the buses were to compete head-to-head with the railway, then the branch line would be put at risk.

With the town's businesses, traders, farmers and workers depending on the trains, closure could prove damaging to the local economy. Perhaps the town's governors have an inkling of how the town may be altered if the roads take over, potentially changing the very fabric of life in this small town.

Working in partnership with BR, the bus service is timed to connect with the sparse passenger services, offering the convenience of quick and comfortable transport to the outlying hamlets and villages that the railway does not reach.

This is an easy facet of 1960s life to recreate in miniature, using either a kit or out of the box depot building and some of the impressive replica buses available. Adding a bus depot certainly makes for an interesting and thought provoking scene, depicting British life on the cusp of change.

Suppliers

Dapol, Evergreen, EFE, Britbus and Corgi products available from model shops

Dart Castings
17 Hurst Close, Staplehurst TN12 0BX
Website: *www.dartcastings.co.uk*
Harburn Hamlet products available from model shops or direct from

Harburn Hobbies
67 Elm Row, Leith Walk, Edinburgh EH7 4AQ
Tel: 0131 556 3233
Website: *www.harburnhobbies.co.uk*

Langley Models
166 Three Bridges Road, Crawley, RH10 1LE
Tel: 01293 516329
Website: *www.langleymodels.co.uk*

Mainly Trains
Unit C South Road Workshops, Watchet TA23 0HF
Tel: 01984 634543
Website: *www.mainlytrains.co.uk*

Spare engines, tyres and lubricating oil are kept safely in a secure yard.

7 In order to achieve a realistic texture to the rendered building Tamiya textured paint can be stippled over the surface, spreading the gritty mixture evenly. The Light Sand shade has been used here, forming a suitable undercoat for the acrylic topcoats. Don't forget to paint the interior in an appropriate shade.

8 To create a realistic flag to adorn the flagpole, Milliput epoxy putty was rolled to a flat shape, before cutting to a rectangle and moulding to a suitably fluttering shape. By wrapping the putty around the pole, a strong bond is achieved. Allow to set overnight before painting.

9 The kit offers a rudimentary set of doors in the form of printed paper components, but a much better representation can be quickly formed from a sheet of modeller's basswood. Cut the various panels to size and score vertical lines to represent the individual planks.

10 In this instance, the doors have been rendered so as to slide in three sections to one side, while the other side hinges inwards and includes a small 'hatch'-style entrance. Painting before fitting is easier and some light washes with dilute acrylics (weathering shades) will highlight the scored plank lines.

11 Clear glazing (fixed with PVA adhesive) and interior details remain to be added. Use has been made of various details from a Scalescenes garage kit given away free in HM23, along with other items built from scratch. Hornby Skale Lighting bulbs have been fixed to the roof with epoxy adhesive.

12 Laying out the scene, with fencing, gates and a small fueling area adds to the sense of realism. The storage yard houses various spare parts, oil barrels and a recovery truck. The Dapol kit offers a choice of self adhesive labels for the signboard, although it's easy to make your own custom sign using a computer.

The timber-sided bus shelter looks the part, especially when suitable figures are added.

Installing third-rail in 'OO'

With the rise in interest in Southern Region third-rail Electric Multiple Units **MIKE WILD** shows what is involved in adding realistic cosmetic third-rails on an 'OO' gauge railway.

Third-rail Electric Multiple Units (EMUs) have gained in popularity recently and especially following the release of Bachmann's superb model of the BR 4-CEP four-car units. Now two more third-rail units are on their way in ready-to-run form covering the BR

2-EPB two-car units and the BR 4-VEP four car units through Bachmann and Hornby respectively.

Until recently anyone wishing to model the third-rail network had to turn to kits for rolling stock and while that is still true for the majority of the EMUs which operated on the Southern,

it is a situation which is gradually changing.

The Southern Region's 750v DC network employed an energised third-rail for electrified routes which EMUs and electric locomotives used to collect the power they needed to move. This network is the most extensive third-rail

system in the UK, the only other location being the Merseyrail network around Liverpool using the same source for power collection.

Unlike the London Underground system, which uses a fourth rail located centrally between the running rails as the current return (the energised rail being on the outside of the running rails on one side only) the Southern Region's return rail is the running rails. As you might imagine the energised third-rail posed a safety risk and still does today because the live rail is at ground level, so if you want to view the third-rail network at work don't even consider wandering off the end of the platform to take a closer look – the consequences could be deadly.

Modelling the third-rail

In model form we can't replicate a fully operational powered third-rail easily (it's a very different proposition indeed from using Hornby Dublo three-rail track, for example), but it is possible to install a cosmetic third-rail using readily available components from Peco. The two main items you need to be aware of are IL-1 Code 60 rail (2ft lengths) and IL-120 conductor rail chairs. The same equipment can be used for models of the London Underground

network, but there is one subtle difference – the number of sleepers between each insulating pot. On the Southern there are five sleepers between each insulating pot and on the Underground the spacing is four sleepers.

The first job in installing third-rail is to ballast and weather the track as required – doing this after the third-rail has been fitted makes life much more complicated. Once this has been done you can move on to the repetitive tasks involved in fitting the conductor rail. This can be broken down into four processes:

■ Painting the tops of insulator pots brown.
■ Threading the code 60 rail onto the insulator pots.
■ Drilling 0.8mm holes in every sixth sleeper.
■ Pushing the insulator pots into the previously drilled holes.

Another important point to consider is the type of track you are using. The Peco insulator pots come with a spacer which can be used to raise the third-rail for use with Peco code 100 track. This spacer must not be used with code 75 track as the extra height will foul the underframes of locomotives. In our view the spacer is best left out

whichever type of track you use as it will increase the necessarily fine clearances for easier running and maintenance of the track.

Hornby Magazine's Bay Street Mk II is fully equipped with a cosmetic conductor rail and the only locomotives we have found to need modification to pass the rail once installed are the Hornby Class 73s. The sandpipes on the bogies of these models are quite wide and the simplest route around this is to remove the sandpipes completely and replace them with fine wire versions which can be inset closer to the running rails to avoid them fouling the conductor rail. Virtually every other locomotive that we have tested has easily coped with clearing the conductor rail.

The installation process is straightforward, but as with all areas of trackwork, care, patience and time are required to make a good job of it. The steps in this feature will guide you through the process and show you exactly how it can be done.

What we used
IL-1 Peco code 60 individulay rail
IL-120 Peco conductor rail chairs
406 Railmatch sleeper grime paint

Installing third-rail on a 'OO' model railway is made simpler with Peco's conductor rail chairs and code 60 rail, but it still takes a little patience. The result though is a realistic railway for EMUs.

Installing third-rail around point work takes care and attention. The diagrams with this feature explain how it works. This is a DC Kits 2-HAP EMU on *Hornby Magazine's* Bay Street Mk II.

Expanding an EMU fleet

With the potential for three ready-to-run Southern Region EMUs being available by the end of 2010 the outlook of the electric modeller is already very good, but if you are looking to further expand your fleet then kit building is the only way forward.

There are several manufacturers producing kits for Southern EMUs including DC Kits, MARC Models, Southern Pride Models and No Nonsense Kits. DC Kits products are straightforward to assemble as the main body construction is from plastic with etched brass and whitemetal details. MARC Models products are produced mainly from etched brass with additional components in whitemetal. No Nonsense Kits products use pre-formed aluminium bodyshells coupled with whitemetal castings and etched brass details and are also reasonably straightforward to assemble. Southern Pride Models kits are formed of pre-printed side and plastic bodyshells.

Beyond these companies there are also others producing components for Southern EMUs including MJT through Dart Castings which produces a range of cast metal cab fronts and etched brass sides for various EMUs.

Through these companies models of the earlier 2-BIL and 2-HAL units can be assembled plus Bulleid pattern BR built 2-EPB and 4-EPB units. Bulleid and BR 4-SUB are available too plus kits for the 2-HAP, 4-EPB, 4-DD double decker and 'Brighton Belle' all Pullman five car sets. Table 1 details the EMUs available ready-to-run and in kit form offering an insight into the myriad of models.

The following steps show how to install Peco's third-rail products in a series of simple steps.

Table 1- EMU models, ready-to-run and kits

EMU	Manufacturer	Notes
BR 4-CEP	Bachmann	Ready-to-run, launched November 2009
BR 4-CEP	DC Kits	Kit, currently available
BR 4-CEP	Southern Pride Models	Kit, currently available – refurbished version
BR 4-BEP	Southern Pride Models	Kit, currently unavailable
BR 2-EPB	Bachmann	Ready-to-run, due for release December 2010
BR 2-EPB	DC Kits	Kit, currently unavailable
BR 2-EPB	Southern Pride Models	Kit, currently available
BR 4-VEP	Hornby	Ready-to-run, due for release late 2010
BR MLV	DC Kits	Kit, currently available
BR MLV	Southern Pride Models	Kit, currently available
Bulleid 2-EPB	No Nonsense Kits	Kit, currently available
BR 4-EPB	DC Kits	Kit, currently available
BR 4-EPB	Southern Pride Models	Kit, currently available
Bulleid 4-EPB	No Nonsense Kits	Kit, currently available
Bulleid 4-SUB	No Nonsense Kits	Kit, currently available
BR 4-SUB	No Nonsense Kits	Kit, currently available
BR 2-HAP	DC Kits	Kit, currently available
BR 2-HAP	Southern Pride Models	Kit, currently available
Bulleid 2-HAP	No Nonsense Kits	Kit, currently available
Bulleid 4-COR	MARC Models	Kit or ready-to-run
6-PAN	MARC Models	Ready-to-run, custom built
6-PUL	MARC Models	Ready-to-run, custom built
2-HAL	MARC Models	Ready-to-run, custom built
4-SUB	MARC Models	Ready-to-run, custom built
BR 4-TC	Southern Pride Models	Kit, currently available
BR 4-REP	Southern Pride Models	Kit, currently available
BR 4-CIG	Southern Pride Models	Kit, currently unavailable
BR 4-BIG	Southern Pride Models	Kit, currently unavailable
BR 4-VEP	Southern Pride Models	Kit, currently unavailable
Pullman 5-BEL	Golden Age Models	Ready-to-run, launched 2010
Pullman 5-BEL	MARC Models	Ready-to-run, custom built

Third-rail positioning

Determining the correct position of the live third-rail on a model railway can be difficult, but by following these simple rules an authentic recreation of the third-rail network can be reproduced.

Stations

At stations the live rail would always be at the furthest point from the platform face. See adjacent diagram.

Crossings

Junctions and crossings are the most complex part of the system as power always needs to be supplied no matter where the train is travelling to or from. The diagram below explains how it works for a simple crossover.

Level crossings

Where the third-rail routes intercepted a public highway or foot crossing the live rail was shielded by wooden shuttering either side. This is difficult to replicate in 'OO' scale, but can be achieved by using plastic micro strip appropriately painted. The shuttering would cover at least 6ft of the live rail from the edge of the crossing.

Yards

In general third-rail was not provided in goods yards. In the case of the larger yards served by electric locomotives the Southern Railway installed overhead electrification and provided its electric locomotives with a pantograph. Following introduction of the Class 73 Electro Diesels the overhead was no longer needed as the 600hp diesel engine could be used to operate the locomotive within a goods yard.

However, EMU carriage sidings required the live rail throughout to power EMUs arriving and departing. As per the road and foot crossings this was usually contained within wooden boards as a safety measure.

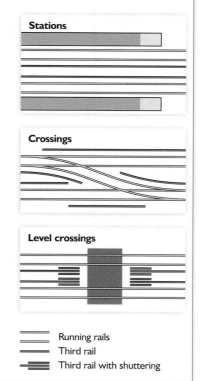

Stations

Crossings

Level crossings

‗‗‗‗ Running rails
──── Third rail
▬▬▬▬ Third rail with shuttering

HOW TO DO IT Installing third-rail for the Southern Region

1 The first job is to paint the tops of the insulator pots. To do this cut away the webbing on the plastic sprue around the head of each pot but leave the pots attached to the centre of the sprue.

2 Using a fine paintbrush and a suitable colour – we turned to our trusted Railmatch Sleeper Grime – paint the tops of each pot. This is best done in batches to avoid the monotony of this repetitive task. Once the paint has fully dried (preferably overnight) cut the insulator pots off the sprue.

3 These can now be threaded onto lengths of code 60 rail individually – 22 are required for a 2ft length.

4 With the insulator pots threaded onto the rail the next job is to drill 0.8mm holes into every sixth sleeper. Alignment is central in the outside section of the sleeper. Rather than using a powered drill, make these holes using a pin vice to avoid damaging the fine drill bit.

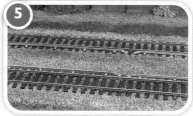

5 With the holes drilled the insulator pots can now be pushed into position. The code 60 rail is quite flexible and installing it on a curve is just as straightforward as on straight track.

6 Painting of the sides of the conductor rail is easier once it is in position. Again we used Railmatch Sleeper Grime to colour the rail sides applied with a fine brush. Should you want to go further, short lengths of single-core wire could be added to the end of each section of conductor rail and linked to the next, as per the prototype.

Tarpaulin
wagons

Adding a tarpaulin to an open goods wagon can create the illusion of varying loads and also cover an area which can then be used to add extra weight to a model. Using Smiths' model tarpaulins, **PHIL PARKER** reveals how to add these finishing touches to your wagons.

Adding a tarpaulin to an open wagon adds greater detail and realism to a model. These Smiths' tarpaulins are readily available from model shops and only take a short time to add to wagons.

You might have noticed that it rains in the UK occasionally and when it does we cover ourselves with waterproof clothes to avoid getting soaked. Faced with the same problem, the railways have since the earliest days chosen to cover up items travelling in open merchandise wagons with waterproof tarpaulins.

Take a look at a photograph of any goods yard and, other than coal, you'll see very few actual wagon loads, but there are an awful lot of mysterious lumps

covered with grey tarpaulins. Unlike models, real railways tried their best not to ship empty wagons around the country as it cost them money. In fact the quickest way to add a bit of variety and realism to a rake of model wagons is to cover them up. Any load that could be damaged by the weather would be sheeted so curvaceous loads of hay or straw would disappear under tarpaulins that would appear a bit like an overstuffed cushion. Rather firmer would be sack loads where part of the reason for a sheet would be to

restrain the load.

Like all things railway, wagon loading was governed by strict instructions which means there are plenty of photographs clearly showing tarpaulins in use. However these are often specially posed so it's better to look at trains on the move for inspiration. Not that any of us need an excuse to study pictures of trains of course.

Tarpaulins weren't considered disposable items. Each would be lettered to show which company it belonged to

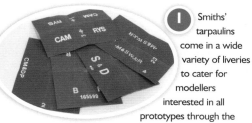

1 Smiths' tarpaulins come in a wide variety of liveries to cater for modellers interested in all prototypes through the ages. In 4mm scale, the BR version is around 82mm x 57mm and made of grey paper printed in white. Straight out of the packet they are a bit clean but this can soon be fixed.

3 To give the tarpaulin a bit of wear I start by screwing it up and then smoothing it out again. In real life they were folded so putting some creases in by doing this isn't a bad idea either. Thread is glued to the back corners with PVA.

5 This stage is easier if you are good at wrapping Christmas presents. At each end you have to fold the sheet in and tie the ropes around the buffers. Since the tarpaulin isn't big enough to cover the end supports for the sheet rail on this model, I used a couple of bits of wire tucked up inside the cover to represent the rail itself. A dose of weathering powders and this wagon is ready for the layout.

7 Sometimes a van with a leaky roof would be covered so it could complete its journey without unloading. They wouldn't run for very long in this state – a quick trip to the repair shops would be in order. It makes a nice change in a rake of vans though. For extra variety, you can also sheet cattle wagons that have been pressed into service as vans during the harvest season when extra carrying capacity would be needed at short notice.

2 A Cooper Craft GWR seven plank open wagon is the candidate I've chosen for covering. In real life the tarpaulin would be supported by a metal rail called a sheet rail. Since this will be hidden I replaced it with a piece of 1mm plasticard as this is stronger than wire. As far as I know there isn't a currently available RTR wagon designed for fitting with a tarpaulin in this way so I'm afraid if you want a pointed top to your wagon, you have to kit build. Paint the wagon before sheeting as working up to the edges of the paper sheet will be tricky at best.

4 Fold the sheet along its length to establish the centre and then glue it to the sides of the wagon with some all purpose glue. Let this dry before moving on to the next stage. Be careful with the glue as it's important to avoid it spreading out of the sides.

6 It's not just wagons supplied with sheet rails that are covered. Anything that could be damaged by the weather was treated in this way so you can also cover open merchandise (not coal or ore) wagons. Before sheeting the wagon it's a good idea to put some sort of shape in the load area. Polystyrene is a good bet for this or pieces of balsa wood.

8 Tarpaulins were transported between stations by loading them into empty wagons. If you need a bit more weight in a model, wrapping a bit of lead sheet in one can be very handy. It wasn't unusual to see several sheets being transported in this way.

and there would also be a unique number printed on it. That would be recorded by the goods clerk and the cost of hiring the sheet would be charged to the customer.

Modelling tarpaulins is strictly a DIY task. There have been a couple of attempts in ready-to-run form but by and large these have been unsuccessful as making a realistic tarpaulin seems to be beyond current manufacturing technology. Don't worry though, it's easy to do.

Smiths' model tarpaulins are available from many suppliers and for just under £4 you get a little packet containing five sheets. If that's too rich for you then some good quality grey paper will work reasonably well.

In BR days the sheets tended to look a bit the worse for wear and so if you dust the model version with weathering powders, the lack of printing won't be immediately obvious.

As well as making your trains look more interesting, covering a fake load is

a handy way of providing a hiding place for a bit of extra weight in a wagon that has turned out lighter than expected. The tarpaulin is also handy for covering up that less-than-perfect paint job you might have carried out. Truly a useful item.

Ready-to-run wagons with sheet rails

Wagon	Manufacturer	Cat No.
12-ton open shock wagon	Bachmann	37-877
Five plank china clay wagon	Bachmann	33-080B

Adding
digital sound
to a 'Super D'

Digital Command Control has brought about a revolution in technology and this is most noticeable in the range of sound equipped locomotives which are now available ready-to-run. But what if the locomotive you want isn't already available with sound fitted? MIKE WILD turns to Howes Models' sound chip catalogue to equip a Bachmann LNWR 'Super D' 0-8-0 with the right noises.

Technology is a wonderful thing. In model railway terms Bachmann and Hornby have embraced this in the form of digital command control and as well as supplying control equipment both are now making DCC fitted and DCC sound fitted locomotives available as catalogue releases.

Bachmann currently offers a selection of DCC fitted locomotives whereas Hornby has taken the route of offering all DCC ready models (those with a decoder socket but no decoder) also available with a decoder factory-installed for a modest extra sum.

All this has made digital control much more accessible. No longer do we have to customise our models by fitting our own chips, although that option is still fully available to those who have a preference of manufacturer for their digital chips.

However, the best of all this is the opportunity to run models with realistic sounds through digital sound decoders. These work like a standard decoder, but on top of the normal control package they offer realistic sounds including user controlled extras which can make the model railway experience all the more realistic and enjoyable.

Bachmann started the sound revolution in British outline 'OO' gauge with its Class 20 and now offers a range of diesel locomotives with sound chips plus in 2010 it launched its first DCC sound fitted steam locomotive – the Stanier 'Jubilee' 4-6-0. Hornby has been quick off the mark too and now has a growing range of sound fitted models which all started with the Stanier 'Duchess' 4-6-2 in 2009.

Table 1 lists all the DCC sound fitted locomotives currently available ready-to-run.

Sourcing your own sounds

If the locomotive you want isn't available with a sound chip then it is time to turn attention to third party chips to do the job for you. Howes Models has been a supporter of digital sound almost since the beginning and it offers a comprehensive range of chips suitable for all manner of locomotives. There are various options too including 8-pin and 21-pin sockets and this is where we turned for our project – the Bachmann 'Super D' 0-8-0.

In terms of installation the 'Super D' is a very straightforward job, but if you don't want to do it yourself then most model shops offer a decoder fitting service for a few extra pounds. One thing to note with digital sound decoders is their cost. These complex pieces of electrical technology can cost almost the same as a ready-to-run locomotive, but their values are clear to see.

The 'Super D' sound decoder produced by Howes is available in two forms – with 'wheeze' and without. Those who know the 'Super Ds' well will have heard the characteristic 'wheeze' that these locomotives emitted in service and the chip we have chosen for this model has that particular feature.

With the 'Super D' having a 21-pin decoder socket, it should be a simple case of 'plug and play' with this sound decoder, but due to the size of the decoder board and the position of pin 1 we had to turn the printed circuit board round inside the tender to allow the decoder to fit within the tender. Pin 1 is denoted by an empty space on the decoder and socket and it takes a matter of moments to remove the blanking plug and install the decoder. However, take care when pushing the decoder onto the pins as they can be damaged easily.

Another point worth noting is the words of caution supplied with the sound decoder for the 'Super D'. In these Howes Models states: "It has been brought to our attention that some of these models may be affected by a fault on the circuit board under the footplate. It would appear that some of the early batch have suffered with solder bleed causing a short circuit on two pins. This is not normally discovered when operating on DC but may become apparent when fitting a DCC decoder."

The model chosen for this project is one of the later batches and we had no issues at all with solder bleed between the pins on the circuit board under the footplate. On the plus side Bachmann has designed the tender of the 'Super D' with digital sound in mind and as well as being factory fitted with a 21-pin decoder socket the tender base is pre-drilled to allow sounds to escape from a speaker hidden inside the tender body reducing the amount of work involved in this installation.

Individual sounds

The Howes Models sound decoder comes with 11 preset sound functions for the 'Super D'. These are:
F1 – sound on/off
F2 – long whistle/hooter
F3 – short whistle/hooter
F4 – buffering up
F5 – coupling up
F6 – injectors
F7 – drain cocks
F8 – buffer clash on wagons
F9 – acceleration/deceleration over ride
F10 – shunting mode
F11 – wheel/track groan

All of these functions can be activated through a digital control handset, although the Lenz Compact for example only offers four function keys, so F5 and above would be inaccessible with this type of basic handset. For our trials we operated the locomotive with a Gaugemaster Prodigy DCC controller which returned superb results. One change we made to the CV settings was to reduce the volume

The completed DCC sound fitted 'Super D' at work on Hornby Magazine's Berrybridge. Externally there is no difference, but the sounds emitted by the locomotive make all the difference.

Contacts

Howes Models
Address: Howes Models, 12 Banbury Road, Kidlington, Oxford OX5 2BT
Tel: 01865 848000
Website: www.howesmodels.co.uk

Bachmann
Website: www.bachmann.co.uk

What we used

Product	Cat No.	Price
Howes Models/ESU sound decoder and speaker (with wheeze)	SS0107A	£115.00
Bachmann 'Super D' 0-8-0 49064, BR black with late crests	31-475A	£92.95

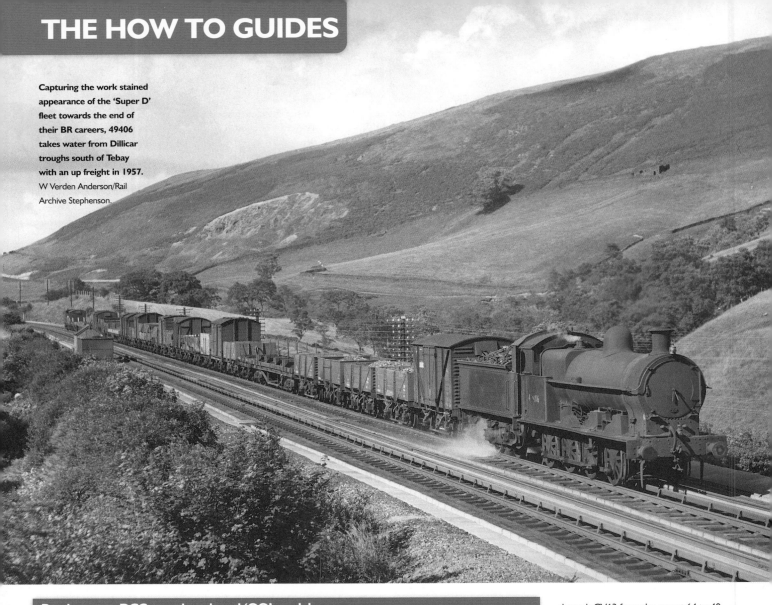

Capturing the work stained appearance of the 'Super D' fleet towards the end of their BR careers, 49406 takes water from Dillicar troughs south of Tebay with an up freight in 1957.
W Verden Anderson/Rail Archive Stephenson.

Ready-to-run DCC sound equipped 'OO' models

Locomotive	Livery	Manufacturer	Cat No.
Class 08 08844	EWS	Hornby	R2902XS*
Class 08 D3105	BR green	Hornby	R2903XS*
Class 20 20034	BR blue	Bachmann	32-035DS
Class 20 D8158	BR green	Bachmann	32-033DS
Class 24 D5100	BR green	Bachmann	32-429DS
Class 25/2 25245	BR blue	Bachmann	32-326DS
Class 25/3 D7638	BR green	Bachmann	32-401DS
Class 31 31247	Railfreight red stripe	Hornby	R2900XS
Class 37/0 37049	BR blue	Bachmann	32-783DS
Class 40 D211 Mauretania	BR green	Bachmann	32-480DS*
Class 45 D55	BR green	Bachmann	32-678DS
Class 47 D1746	BR green	Bachmann	32-801DS
Class 50 50015 Valiant	Dutch	Hornby	R2802XS
Class 50 50037 Illustrious	Large logo blue	Hornby	R2901XS
Class 60 60042 The Hundred of Hoo	EWS	Hornby	R2899XS
Class 66 66702 Blue Lightning	GBRf	Bachmann	32-727DS
Collett 'Castle' 4098 Kidwelly Castle	BR green	Hornby	R2897XS
Gresley 'A4' 60001 Sir Ronald Matthews	BR green	Hornby	R2896XS
Maunsell 'Schools' 30909 St Pauls	BR black	Hornby	R2898XS*
Stanier 'Black Five' 44875	BR black	Hornby	R2895XS
Stanier 'Duchess' 46240 City of Coventry	BR maroon	Hornby	R2894XS
Stanier 'Jubilee' 45593 Kolhapur	BR green	Bachmann	31-177DS

* Catalogue numbers marked with an asterisk had not been released at the time of publication, but were expected before the end of 2010.

Note: Further livery and number variations are available on some of the models listed above from shop stocks – these items being no longer listed in current catalogues.

through CV63 from the preset 64 to 40 to improve performance of the speaker.

Overview

The installation of this sound decoder is very straightforward and takes a matter of minutes after familiarising yourself with the components. The end result is a realistic sound package connected to a high quality speaker which doesn't suffer from any distortion at all.

Howes DCC sound decoders are well worth exploring, although it should be noted that some require more work to install than others – the 'Super D' chip being a prime example of the simplest installations. If you've been hankering after a particular locomotive with sound, give it a try – it is well worth the cost and time to install.

Tools required

The only tool required for this installation is a set of jewellers' screw drivers with a crosshead screw driver being the required tool to release the tender body from the chassis and also the printed circuit board inside the tender.

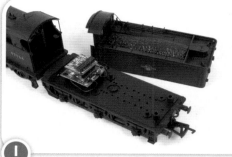

1 The first step is to remove the tender body. This is achieved by removing the two small crosshead screws at the rear of the tender. The body clips in at the front and once lifted reveals the 21-pin DCC decoder socket and pre-drilled holes for the sound to escape.

2 With the tender body removed the 21-pin blanking plug can be removed from the decoder socket. Take care to lift this vertically to avoid damaging the pins of the socket.

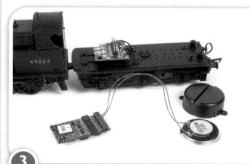

3 The Howes Models decoder comes with a suitable speaker factory fitted to the decoder circuit board. Be careful when handling the wires. A speaker enclosure (far right) is also included.

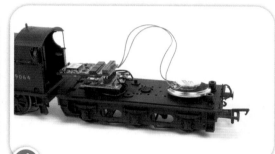

4 With the printed circuit board in its factory position the new decoder won't fit inside the tender body as illustrated here. The simplest route to rectify this is to turn the tender circuit board through 180 degrees.

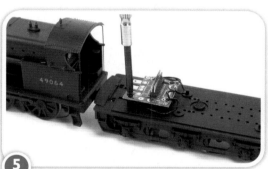

5 To turn the tender circuit board and decoder socket undo the single crosshead screw and then rotate the board. The two locating lugs fit perfectly the other way round too.

6 With the circuit board and decoder socket turned round the chip can be fitted directly onto the pins taking care to note the missing pin on both the decoder and socket for correct positioning. At this point the speaker is simply laid in place for testing which is a good idea at this point to check the installation – the factory preset address for the decoder is address 3.

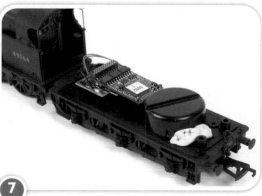

7 The speaker enclosure can now be added over the top of the speaker. Just in case future maintenance is required we fixed the enclosure in place with blue tack. The same material was used to keep the speaker wires neat and tidy.

8 The locomotive is now ready for the tender to be refitted and test running. The only changes we made to the factory setting on the decoder were to reduce the output volume from 64 to 40 through CV63.

Building a
micro layout

Micro layouts have become popular with those short of space for a model railway as well for quick projects. **PHIL PARKER** describes how he went about building Melbridge Parva – a 730mm x 200mm micro layout in 'OO' gauge.

Inspirations for layouts come from many places. Melbridge Parva started with a plastic box on sale at the Midlands Model Engineering exhibition from the BB Engineering Services stand. I looked at it a few times during the show and wondered if I could build a layout inside it. At 73cm long and 20cm wide, it was certainly a larger canvas than the box files I'd used for the Melbridge Box Company (HM25). Melbridge Box Company was great fun to build and surprisingly popular with exhibition visitors to boot so I fancied a sequel. Chatting to the stall holder, I mentioned my ideas and he promptly handed over a box for no charge. From this point on I had no choice but to have a go.

Micro layouts are very fashionable right now. Several books and websites are devoted to the subject. Lack of space in modern homes or perhaps a desire for instant gratification has persuaded more and more people to experiment with something of a modest size before embarking on a more major project. Chatting to exhibition visitors when displaying the Box Company, lots

of people are really interested and say nice things about it, although I wonder how many really go away and do something similar themselves. Perhaps it's like reading recipe books; good fun but it all looks too much work so you still order a takeaway.

I am a big fan of micro layouts for one simple reason – I get bored easily.

None of my layouts are large, even the 'proper' ones are no more than 9ft long. When my father and I tried to build a whopping 18ft long continuous run model we got tired of it after a few years and sold it. The trouble is that every job on a big model seems to take forever. People say that they are going to spend the next year ballasting the

A Hunslet 0-4-0 diesel shunter propels a pair of wagons into the sidings for loading.

A Fowler 0-6-0T shunts wagons for loading at Melbridge Parva.

track and I wonder why. It's a desperately tedious job in my view. This is supposed to be a hobby; if I want boredom, that's what the day job provides.

The positives

Looking at it more positively, if you are a new modeller then a micro project is a good starting point. Every technique I used to produce Melbridge Parva is the same as I'd use on a bigger project. If it didn't work I'd simply throw it away without having lost much time or money.

An overall view of Melbridge Parva showing its compact make up.

On that basis, when the time comes to build the big railway then you'll already know what works and what doesn't. This layout is utterly conventional, just small. Points are operated by Seep solenoid motors. Power comes via a Gaugemaster DC handheld controller. Track is hand built because I had the bits in stock but it would have been easier to use Peco products.

Anyway, I started with a box. Before I went any further I needed a plan. Now I am good at many activities within this hobby but devising track plans is not one of them. After messing around with some Hornby planning diagrams I still hadn't produced anything that looked interesting. At this point I wrote up the problem on my blog (www.philsworkbench.co.uk) and struck

lucky. Michael Campbell spotted the post and on his blog (www.michaelsrailways.blogspot.com) put up three different plans to fit the space. Each looked very promising, certainly better than my efforts, and so I cut out some full-size point plans and arranged them on a board to get a better idea what they would look like. I'm very grateful to Michael for his effort, I'm not sure how this model would have turned out without him. Needless to say when I showed him a photograph of the finished version, he pointed out that I'd actually built a hybrid of two of the plans. Just like me not to read instructions.

This wasn't the only part of the project I had internet help with. Struggling for a layout name I put out an appeal on the Double O Gauge Association forum and within a day was inundated with suggestions. I'd stipulated that the name had to include Melbridge, fictional location of the film *Random Harvest* and where many of my models are based. Pondering the ideas for a few weeks, it seemed that Melbridge Parva suggested a bucolic location amusingly at odds with the model I had built. Thanks to Tony Newton for his suggestion.

As an working model, obviously Melbridge Parva has its limitations. You can operate it as a shunting puzzle by using six wagons and trying to

reorganise them within the space available in the classic Inglenook fashion. It makes a handy test track too for any new models I build since the track is the same as that on the bigger layouts. However, I certainly wouldn't want to spend two days operating it at an exhibition!

Still, as a shunting puzzle it can be a great source of entertainment at home for half an hour or so at a time, depending on how complicated the shunting movements become, and it is also particularly practical from this view point. As a layout it takes a matter of minutes to set up meaning that it doesn't have to be a permanent fixture in the home. This fact alone is another of the great plus points for a micro layout as setting up a larger layout and only running it once in a blue moon before packing it away again can be a strain. From the fun angle, this makes micro layouts very attractive.

The build

The overall dimensions of Melbridge Parva are 730mm x 200mm with a maximum height of 140mm. This can all be contained within the single plastic box I obtained and allows the lid to be kept on to keep the model covered when in storage or transit. This is particularly worthwhile if you have pets as it stops the ingress of loose fur which is often a problem with pet owners' model railways.

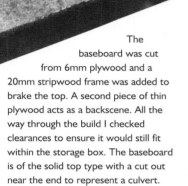

plan marked on it and set about building the track as described in HM33's Parker's Guide. A couple of hours were spent tweaking the track after it was built for perfect running by

the model the mortar was added first with a slightly thinned Humbrol enamel followed by brick colouring using Derwent

Artists pencil crayons rubbed on the surface. The best colours in my view are Copper Beech, Terracotta and Venetian Red.

The next building along is an anonymous corrugated structure set on top of a few rows of bricks. This was finished in a basic green colour before further variations of colour and tone were added on top to add texture to the finished structure.

There are two further buildings on Melbridge Parva which some may recognise. The first is half of a Hornby Skaledale colliery building which was separated into two halves with a junior hacksaw. This was repainted to match the rest of the buildings and adds an additional structure quickly to the layout. The final building is the classic Airfix single road locomotive shed. With the tooling now being 40 years old it took a bit of work, but with interior detailing, a high quality paint finish and thinned down window frames.

The fine ballast used on industrial lines has been produced using left over sawdust from sanding a wooden floor. After being glued in place is was painted with Precision Paints frame dirt colour. Other textures are made up with DIY filler smeared with a palette knife, Greenscene textured paint, Heiki puffer grass and various grass coloured flocks.

To create a small fiddle yard I made a small baseboard from the same materials as the main board. This plugs into the

The baseboard was cut from 6mm plywood and a 20mm stripwood frame was added to brake the top. A second piece of thin plywood acts as a backscene. All the way through the build I checked clearances to ensure it would still fit within the storage box. The baseboard is of the solid top type with a cut out near the end to represent a culvert.

To devise the plan I used a selection of SMP paper point templates and a selection of wagons and a locomotive to gauge how much room would be needed on each track to accommodate various combinations of locomotive and wagons. Once the plan had been finalised I subcontracted the track construction to my dad. He pinned the sleepers to softwood with the track

running a handful of wagons around the track by hand. This is one of the advantages of PCB board track – it can be adjusted infinitely, so there is always a case for having a go with this type of track construction. Next up holes for the point motors and magnets for the Spratt & Winkle uncoupling magnets were created before the track was glued in place for the final time.

The buildings on Melbridge Parva are all scratch built using my usual card shell method covered with suitable embossed plasticard. The first to be built was the brick warehouse which is based on a 7mm scale layout called Wood Street. The plan was sketched out on the card using plastic window frames as a guide and after a little reworking the end result is a good looking half relief building which serves its purpose. It has been covered with Slaters Plasticard Flemish bond brick plasticard before further detailing with window arch tops and painting. To paint

HOW TO DO IT **Building Melbridge Parva**

1 This is the box. The internal dimensions are 730 x 200 x 140cm. Big enough for rolls of wrapping paper apparently. At the ends there are clips to hold the lid in place and stop inquisitive cats from looking in.

2 The baseboard top was cut from 6mm plywood. SMP point plans were cut out and placed on top to help planning. A couple of wagons and a Bachmann junior locomotive gave an idea of siding space. In the end I decided on one of Michaels plans and jiggled the precise arrangement to get as much as possible out of the limited space.

A Yorkshire Class 02 shunts a single wagon load of ballast past the engine shed.

main layout with lengths of brass tube and rod soldered to copperclad board either side of the join. Peco track was laid on this section as it saved a lot of time and effort when it wasn't required.

Almost finished

The model is nearly finished but I think there is still possibilities for further work. There are areas where a bit of extra detail would be beneficial. For example, some sack trucks on the loading bay would be nice. Maybe a little extra detail inside the engine shed too, I'm sure the miniature work force would appreciate a workbench. One omission is figures. I'm not sure whether I should add them or not. At the moment I think it looks better without but maybe one day I'll change my mind. That's the beauty of this hobby though, there is always something to do.

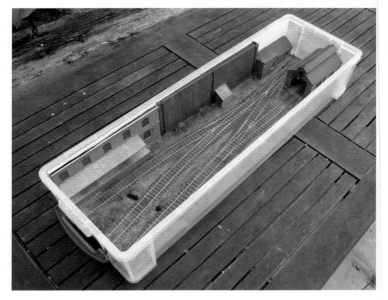

The whole scenic section fits within a 730mm x 200mm storage box which keeps it free from dust and out of harm's way when stored.

Melbridge Parva track plan

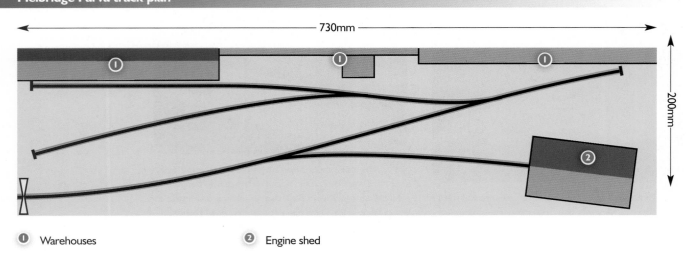

① Warehouses   ② Engine shed

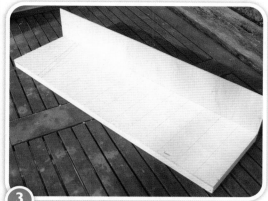

3 A framework of 20mm strip wood braces the top and another piece of thin ply acts as a backscene. At this point I checked that it would all go back in the box with the lid on – and was relieved when it did. A cheap mitre block ensured sufficient accuracy for my woodworking. A depth of 20mm is just enough space to allow the point motors to be fitted and not get squashed. It's also why I used Seep in preference to Peco, these are a lot deeper and would have left me with less vertical space for scenery.

5 Track construction was subcontracted to my Dad. He pinned the sleepers to a piece of softwood with the trackplan marked on it. HM33 covered the basics of making track from SMP code 75 rail. What you don't see is the couple of hours spent tweaking the track to perfect the running. There was quite a bit of moving wagons around, mostly because we were out of practice adjusting track. Another advantage of a micro layout, you get practice. If I were to lay more track, it would be perfect first time. Probably.

The track was laid on a 2mm thick cork. This wasn't to keep the noise down but to allow more landscaping. I only glued it down where there was track planning to cut any excess away later.

8 I'm using Spratt & Winkle couplings which are uncoupled with small rectangular permanent magnets so took the opportunity to cut holes for these before gluing the track down. To work out where they should be I used a couple of wagons, ironically neither with the correct couplings on, and figured out how close to the point they could be without hitting each other. You can of course fit the magnets after tracklaying as they are narrow enough to go between the rails.

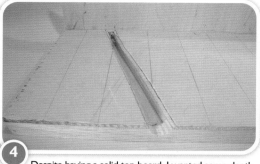

4 Despite having a solid top board, I wanted some depth to the model. Some scrap wood under the board allowed me to cut away a culvert. The advantage of using thin plywood is that this sort of cutting can be carried out with a Stanley knife rather than a saw. A rasp was very handy to for this job as it chewed away the wood quickly and easily. I wasn't too worried at this stage about accuracy as the final shaping would be carried out with filler.

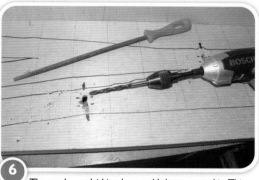

6 The track was laid in place and I drew around it. This allowed me to take it away and cut slots for the point motor rods. A hole saw drill bit (you work it up and down while drilling to turn a hole into a slot) and a rasp were my tools of choice for this.

7

9 All the buildings use my usual card covered with plasticard method of construction. The first to be built was a brick warehouse based on a model seen on the 7mm scale layout Wood Street. The plan was sketched out on the card using some plastic windows as a guide. After a bit of adjustment and re-drawing I came up with this. This was left on the layout for a couple of days and I kept looking at it to see if it looked right.

A 'Z5' 0-4-2T pauses in the shed for a little light maintenance.

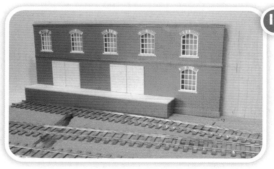

10 Happy with the proportions, Slaters Flemish bond plasticard was glued over the surface with a solvent-free all-purpose glue. Left overnight to dry with a pile of magazines on top, this seems to survive very well over time. Some of my models built this way have lasted the best part of a decade so expansion of different materials doesn't seem to be a problem. Around the top of the windows the arch is formed from small rectangles of cardboard called computer chads. These stopped being produced thirty years ago (unless anyone knows better) but cutting card by hand wouldn't be too much of a chore, for a small number of windows anyway.

11 To colour the brickwork, I used a simple trick picked up at a show a few years ago. The mortar is painted with slightly thinned Humbrol enamel. Once dry, Derwent Artists pencil crayons are rubbed on the surface to colour the brick faces. Copper Beech, Terracotta and Venetian Red seem to work best. This method is far easier than trying to dry-brush paint to do the same thing as the colour doesn't get in the mortar lines.

12 In the middle of the layout I wanted an anonymous plain wall. A simple card rectangle was covered with Wills corrugated iron. A few rows of bricks at the base keep the metalwork out of the damp. A basic green colour was painted over the whole wall and then variations were added by painting individual sheets with the base colour mixed with a touch of yellow, pale green or brown.

13 For the end of the layout I wanted a little building and couldn't decide what to make. Half an hour spent in my local model shop (Classic Train and Motor Bus of Leamington) with a ruler and I found a Skaledale model that was nearly right. Well, it was the right length but too wide. No problem, a few minutes' work with a junior hacksaw split it in half. The section I wanted was painted in the same way as the warehouse so it fitted in with the overall look of the layout.

15 Inside the shed is an inspection pit. According to my friendly experts, these are 3ft 6in deep. Mine had to plug into a hole made between the rails in the shed area hence the top half is just plasticard. A slightly wonky plasticard staircase at one end allows access. If I'd had an Airfix footbridge to hand I'd have used some steps from that instead.

18 I like to brighten up odd corners of grimy industry with a few wild flowers. The tall purple ones are a single bristle dipped in PVA and then into purple flock. The result looks pretty and reasonably convincing. The deeper mounds of green are a scenic mesh intended for trees teased out, glued down and then flocked.

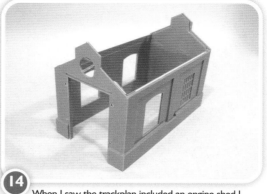

14 When I saw the trackplan included an engine shed I knew only the classic Airfix kit would do the job. However, a forty year old kit wasn't really going to be up to the standards of today. At the very least an interior was required and that meant packing the walls inside flat with 1mm and 2mm plasticard followed by some brick sheet. The biggest problem is that the kit has stretcher bond brickwork with over scale bricks. Inside I used the same sheets as elsewhere and hope no one notices the difference. With the inside lined, I also had to thin down the window mouldings with some fine sandpaper so they didn't stick out either side.

16 To represent the fine ballast of most industrial lines I used some sawdust left over from sanding a wooden floor. This was painted with Precision frame dirt colour. The rest of the ground contours are ready-mixed DIY filler smeared around with a palette knife. Some Greenscene textured paint followed by brown emulsions supplied a nice muddy base colour.

17 Greenery is mostly formed from Heiki puffer grass. On top of this I spray cheap hair lacquer and then sprinkle various colours of flock. It's amazing how quickly this process completely changes the look of the layout. I don't think it took more than a couple of hours to change most of the ground colour from brown to green.

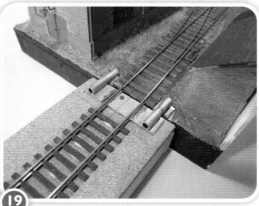

19 For a fiddle yard I made a small baseboard from the same materials as the main version. It plugs into the layout with some lengths of brass tube soldered to a strip of copperclad.

BR's
Eastern
region

The Eastern Region might be the least represented by
ready-to-run models, but it hasn't stopped its popularity.
We take a look at five of the best Eastern Region layouts
from past and future issues of *Hornby Magazine*.

A Gresley 'A4' 4-6-2 thunders through the station and overtakes a goods in the charge of a BR '4MT' 2-6-4T. Mike Wild.

Gresley 'A4' 60027 *Merlin* approaches Scarworth Junction. On the high ground behind the stately home can be seen through the trees. Mike Wild.

Scarworth Junction

Scarworth Junction, also known as the North of England Line by its builders, is the Scarborough and District Railway Modellers first venture into 'N' exhibition layouts. This entertaining steam era layout set, as the group say, 'somewhere in the north of England' was started in 2003 when two members suggested that the club branch out into 'N' gauge. Between them they owned a large amount of stock so to suit this a theme was developed which allowed it to be used in a variety of periods. However, the fictitious location was firmly set in the North of England and the motive power – normally Eastern and Midland stock – reflects this.

At exhibitions the team operate the layout with either pre-nationalisation or post-nationalisation rolling stock with each day of a two-day event being one or the other. This helps continuity and also offers variety to the operators themselves.

The scenic side of the layout features several interesting features including a scratch built stately home on the hillside above the railway at one end, a large station with three through platforms and two bay platforms, a canal side transfer shed and an imposing bridge carrying two separate routes across a river in the shadow of a walled town.

One of the advantages of 'N' gauge is the ability to run scale length trains unhindered and Scarworth Junction makes the most of that potential. At 18ft long and 3ft wide this layout is no box room layout, but this also means that 40 wagon goods and 12 coach trains are perfectly possible without them looking out of place. Trains range from the very latest Bachmann and Dapol offerings to detailed Graham Farish products, scratch built formations (including the LNER 'Silver Jubilee' express) and kit built rolling stock.

The layout is operated from three control panels, one each for the Up and Down lines and the third for the scenic area, branch line and goods yard. The electrics for the layout are conventional analogue DC using four Gaugemaster handheld controllers, one each for the main lines, another for the branch line and the last to shunt the goods yard. There is also a panel mounted controller on each of the Up and Down control panels to assist in shunting the fiddle yards.

Scarworth Junction doesn't run to a timetable as the aim is to keep something running at all times and keep the public interested in the layout when exhibiting. All stock is run in rotation from the fiddle yard which can hold 18 trains, with a further three on the branch line.

The layout is now all but complete, but even so the group still have further plans including adding further detail to the signalling system and also enjoy the hard work they have put into creating the layout.

Opposite page: A 'B17' 4-6-0 leads a van train across the river on the approach to Scarworth Junction. On the branch a Class 108 departs in the opposite direction. Mike Wild.

Scarworth Junction statistics	
Owner:	Scarborough and District RM
Scale:	'N'
Length:	18ft
Width:	3ft
Track:	Peco code 55
Period:	1930s or 1950s North Eastern Region
Featured:	HM33

A BTH Class 15 approaches Bawdsey with banana vans for the warehouse. **Mike Wild.**

Bawdsey

Not everyone has the time to build a layout and when the late Chris Matthewman's East Anglian 'EM' gauge Strove became available, Paul Marshall-Potter faced the challenges of taking on a brilliant and much loved artefact.

Like so many railway modellers, his interest was inherited from his father. If you've been in the hobby for about 15 years or so and visited exhibitions on the northern circuit in the first half of the

1990s, this layout may seem familiar to you. It was built by the late Chris Matthewman as Strove, and took part in 21 exhibitions under his ownership.

Paul visited Roy Jackson and his 'EM' gauge layout regularly, and on one of his running days David Woodward had some locomotives for sale from Chris Matthewman's estate. Whilst talking to David he was advised that David was helping with the estate sale after Chris had died, and Paul asked what had happened to Strove as he'd seen the layout once and had been considering making an East Anglian branch line. It was available and with the family's blessing he arranged a sale.

Having bought Strove, Paul had firm ideas of what he wanted to change to make the previously 1930s period layout suit his penchant for the 1950s and 1960s transition era. The buildings and

structures have all remained unchanged from Chris' original work with a few subtle changes being made revolving around resigning the station, removing the horse drawn vehicles and adding more 'modern' lorries and cars. The signalbox has been left in its pre-nationalisation colours as a remnant of the previous era – this being partly decided by the complexities of repainting the building in situ. Strove has also been renamed Bawdsey to suit its new position in history.

Bawdsey is built to 'EM' gauge standards so all of the rolling stock which operates on the layout has been converted from Paul's already established fleet of kit built wagons together with ready-to-run locomotives, carriages and multiple units. To represent the intended period motive power comprises two Bachmann Class 24s, a pair of Heljan

Bawdsey statistics	
Owner:	Paul-Marshall Potter
Scale:	'EM' (4mm:1ft)
Length:	9ft
Width:	18in
Track:	Handbuilt to 18mm gauge
Period:	1959, BR Eastern Region
Featured:	HM40

A Class 08 shunts the yard as a Class 108 departs Bawdsey. Mike Wild.

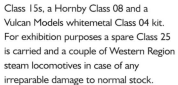

Class 15s, a Hornby Class 08 and a Vulcan Models whitemetal Class 04 kit. For exhibition purposes a spare Class 25 is carried and a couple of Western Region steam locomotives in case of any irreparable damage to normal stock.

The Class 24s have had quite a bit of work done to them. They were used to develop Shawplan laser cut glazing (as was the Hornby 08) and they also have had roof panels changed and new exhausts fitted, as the Bachmann roof is a compromise from Class 24 and Class 25.

Topping off the transformation is an updated version of the operating sequence developed by Chris Matthewman. This has been altered to allow DMU passenger services as well as locomotive hauled workings while the majority of other movements have continued as planned before but with different rolling stock.

A Class 105 waits between duties at Bawdsey. Mike Wild.

A busy scene at Marshmoor as a 'B17' 4-6-0 departs while an 'A3' 4-6-2 approaches the station running parallel with a Class 108 DMU. Mike Wild.

Marshmoor

Ipswich Railway Modellers Association's oldest layout is Marshmoor, a 40ft long 'OO' gauge model with plenty of flexibility to portray different eras and located on BR's Eastern Region. It is well into its 17th year, having been started in 1993 when the association was based in St Peter's Church, Ipswich.

The layout can play host to any number of types and periods of stock because of its neutral architecture and landscape. It is very easy to go from 1940s LNER/LMS to BR blue by strategically placing vehicles and sundries that when paired with the appropriate stock place the layout in a distinctive time period. So a few cars, a change of telephone box and a few road signs later and you can go from running LNER liveried 'J39' 0-6-0s to BR blue Class 31s on a goods train as quick as you like.

The group which operates and maintains Marshmoor has a wide range of interests and as such period 'dressing' sessions are held in order to provide variety and cater to everyone's interest. What Marshmoor offers is a substantial double track main line with a large goods yard, a branch line, a main line station with four platform faces, a locomotive shed (complete with a coaling tower and four-road shed building) and all the entertainment the operating team need. There is a large fiddle yard to the rear and to increase its appeal during operating sessions, and to keep the growing number of diesel modellers satisfied, a diesel depot has been constructed which has its own separate control panel.

The stock is drawn from the operating group and at any one time you can see up to 100 locomotives as well as a whole host of coaches and wagons – the yards when full of wagons look particularly impressive.

With this many trains to be seen it's not surprising that all manufacturers are very well represented from the usual suspects and some very old names come up in conversation too – a Kitmaster LMS Beyer Garrett 2-6-0+0-6-2 being one of the latest and most impressive additions to the roster. The full range of ready-to-run and kit-built examples complements each other and provides the viewing public with a large variety of movement.

To give a flavor of the intent with Marshmoor, imagine a holiday train entering the station on a hot summer Saturday, passengers scattered over the crowded platforms having woken at dawn and packed enough things in case of rain. The guard blows his whistle and the industrial grime of Marshmoor that fills the town's air is replaced by the acrid nose-tickling fumes bellowing from the train (steam or diesel according to preference!). Those holiday train journeys were as English as fish and chips, and the group wanted to create the same sense of anticipation and excitement there used to be on such occasions.

Marshmoor represents a wonderful example of social history by carrying forward into the future those memories and emotions of all who play a part in capturing childhood dreams of running the railway. Long after they've passed on, their cultural and personal memories will live on in a very real sense on this layout.

The association intends to maintain Marshmoor as its centrepiece layout for some time to come. As with any layout it's never finished, there are always repairs, enhancements and improvements to make and this keeps the operating group busy.

A work stained 'WD' 2-8-0 is held in the goods loop outside Marshmoor. Mike Wild.

A Gresley 'A3' at the head of a rake of Gresley teak coaches rounds the curve on the approach to Marshmoor. Mike Wild.

A 'J38' 0-6-0 leaves Flockburgh with a mixed goods. Mike Wild.

Flockburgh

Regarded by many as a dead scale, 3mm:1ft is still kept going by dedicated modellers who appreciate its possibilities. Phil Parker and his father dipped their toes in the water with this finescale Scottish seaside resort which offers a different option for those prepared to stand out and try an alternative scale.

The purchase of a Triang 'Jinty' 0-6-0T years ago had sparked an interest in 3mm:1ft scale railways for Phil and his father which eventually lead to joining the 3mm Society. This gives access to a surprisingly large range of kits and materials. Since Phil had built more than a few etched locomotives and wagons – not least through his Parker's Guide series in *Hornby Magazine* – he decided to have a go at a layout in this unusual but versatile scale. Initial ideas centred around Ballachulish and other Scottish stations but these needed quite a bit of space and a smaller project was needed to test the water.

Flockburgh began life as a plan in an old *Model Railways* magazine. It's as conventional as you get with a fiddle yard at one end running into a terminus station at the other and is set at the end of a branch line on the border between England and Scotland. Armed with a bag of Peco track you could do the same thing in 'OO' in a weekend and have your stock running fairly quickly afterwards. It would undoubtedly be lots of fun, but probably not that appealing to exhibition managers.

The imaginary history to Flockburgh assumes the town was developed as a northern rival to Blackpool without much success. There are a few holidaymakers and a modest amount of goods traffic from the port but nothing to justify facilities greater than a single platform. Like Ventnor on the Isle of Wight, the station area had to be created using dynamite in a hillside, hence the constrained proportions.

Despite the new scale much of the construction is based on previous layouts built by the Parkers. The baseboards are 9mm plywood cut to size by a local wood yard and held together with demountable hinges. The track is code 60 SMP rail soldered to copper-clad sleepers. Point control is by Peco motors and a Gaugemaster controller runs the locomotives.

Despite all this experience, actually building Flockburgh proved more challenging than expected. Since all the rolling stock had to be built they decided to use the finest of the gauges supported by the 3mm Society, 14.2mm, instead of the traditional 12mm used by Triang and many others which offers a fully accurate track spacing rather than the 4ft offered

by standard 12mm gauge track. This resulted in a steep learning curve for people used to the loose tolerances available to the 'OO' modeller.

All the rolling stock is kit-built – no re-worked Triang here! Locomotives are etched brass and usually run on 3mm Society finescale wheels. Anything with six or more wheels sits on a compensated chassis as this seems to be essential to keep it on the track. Diesels are a bit easier thanks to the re-gauged Sharman 'OO' wheels allowed by hiding the overscale flanges behind the sideframes. Wagons come from the superb Parkside range available through the 3mm Society.

Buildings are based on those from the Cawood, Wistow and Selby branch line in North Yorkshire. Daler board shells are covered with plasticard and topped with Wills slate roof materials. Again, this is all based on Phil and his Dad's 4mm experience. In fact many of the components are from the larger scale yet look fine in this application. One area of innovation is right at the front of the model where you find a line of beach huts. Rather than build 13 of them individually a master was made in plasticard and then the rest were cast in polyester resin. Each model has been personalised with different roof and door materials as well as varying degrees of decrepitude.

Despite the trying times of assembling the track and making this 14.2mm gauge layout work Flockburgh has been a great source of pleasure for both of its builders.

Flockburgh statistics	
Owner:	Phil Parker
Scale:	3mm:1ft (14.2mm gauge)
Length:	9ft
Width:	18in
Track:	Hand built with code 60 rail
Period:	BR 1950s/1960s Scottish Region
Featured:	HM32

Viewed across the goods yard the branch passenger working departs as a 'J50' 0-6-0T shunts wagons for the pick up goods. Mike Wild.

Above: In the shadow of the Pennines and EM2 Co-Co passes through Deepcar with an express.
Mike Wild.

Main picture: An EM1 Bo-Bo leads empty steel flats through Deepcar.
Mike Wild.

Deepcar

The Woodhead route between Sheffield Victoria and Manchester Piccadilly was a unique railway. From 1954 the entire route was worked by overhead electric locomotives operating from a 1500v DC overhead system using specially designed locomotives. It character was unique, its locomotives special and its terrain unforgiving.

The Nottingham (Bulwell) Model Railway Society set out to replicate this wonderful railway in 4mm scale more than two decades ago with their model of Deepcar. It is one of few exhibition layouts to feature scale working 1500v DC pattern catenary, although it is actually powered at 12v DC. The layout has been built by the members of the Society and can represent any period between 1955 and 1981.

The overhead electrification is totally scratch built with the EM1 Bo-Bo and EM2 Co-Co electrics using the overhead line as a common return with power also being drawn from the running rails. The station at Deepcar is the basis, located just to the West of Sheffield, and while it closed many years ago the platforms and buildings remained in place long after closure. Deepcar served as a junction for the Stocksbridge railway – a private line which ran from Deepcar to a nearby steelworks and this has been represented on the layout with

connecting trains arriving and departing from the associated yards around the station.

The scenery around Deepcar was extremely steep and the Woodhead route was built with a gentle gradient in mind to allow heavy goods trains to cross the Pennine's. Its main source of traffic was coal to serve power stations and the summit of the line was at the eastern end of Woodhead Tunnel just under 20 miles from Sheffield.

Deepcar represents typical workings on the line in a variety of periods. For these photographs it was placed in the late 1950s and early 1960s offering both BR black and BR green electric locomotives as well as a smattering of diesel power.

This wonderful and historical layout is to be featured in a future issue of *Hornby Magazine* ahead of the Nottingham (East Midlands) Model Railway Exhibition in March 2011 which

will feature an overhead and third-rail electric theme.

Deepcar statistics	
Owner:	Nottingham (Bulwell) MRS
Scale:	'OO'
Length:	26ft
Width:	11ft
Track:	Hand built
Period:	1955-1981
Featured:	Future feature layout

The Electric Revolution

One of the outstanding success stories of the Modernisation Plan was the electrification of the West Coast Main Line and its introduction to Britain of lightweight high-powered Bo-Bo electric locomotives. **EVAN GREEN-HUGHES** traces the history of these groundbreaking designs which were introduced over 50 years ago.

AL1 E3016 passes Tring with an up express for London Euston on May 1 1966. Brian Stephenson.

In the years of post-war austerity most of Britain's railway system was much as it had been for two decades. Express train times remained at the levels of 20 years previously, stations were dirty and poorly maintained and railways were no match for the challenge being posed by roads and domestic airlines.

While the introduction of diesels had stemmed some of the losses and had helped to bring passengers back to the trains, the locomotives in use at that time were only slightly more powerful than the recently withdrawn steam engines.

Where electric traction existed it had been applied mostly to suburban lines, where rapid acceleration and high utilisation had been useful in improving commuter services. The only attempt at overhead electric main line working was on the line from Sheffield and Wath to Manchester which had been opened for business in stages during the early 1950s using a 1500v DC overhead system, which required weighty equipment and gantries to support the supply wires. The system also meant that locomotives were relatively heavy for any given power output.

Ironically British Railways, which had been relatively untouched by enemy action, was lagging in its renewals behind the railways of continental Europe, many of which had required total rebuilding following the conflict, and many of which had adopted electrification wholeheartedly as a way of increasing train speeds and of cutting long-term costs.

West Coast plans

When the Modernisation Plan was announced electrification of the West Coast Main Line was the only scheme of its type to be included. The plan did not propose merely electrifying the route between London Euston and Liverpool/Manchester, but instead proposed completely upgrading the permanent way, stations, signalling and rolling stock to provide the country's first modern line.

Before any serious work could begin a decision had to be made on the electrical system which was to be used. Under the direction of S Warder, the Chief Electrical Engineer of British Railways, consideration was given as to whether to continue with 1500v DC or to plump for the relatively untried 25kV AC system, which in recent tests in France seemed to offer considerable advantages but which presented greater technical challenges, not least in that no one in the UK had any experience of building or working on such a system.

Mr Warder found that there were considerable advantages with the 25kV system, particularly regarding the costs of construction of the overhead itself. As far as locomotives were concerned, although both types cost about the same, there were advantages with those working on the higher voltage. The 25kV locomotive did not waste any power in supplying resistances for speed control and better adhesion resulting from more advanced power systems enabled lighter locomotives to be constructed for a given

AL6 E3112 passes Watford Junction with an up car train in October 1965. C Coles/Rail Archive Stephenson

power output. Not surprisingly the decision went the way of high voltage AC and British Railways began to draw up a specification for suitable motive power.

The design for what were to be the UK's first 95 high-speed 25kV main line locomotives was influenced by several factors. At the top of the list was the British Railways Board's assertion that the days of the loose-coupled freight train were numbered and with them went the need for specialised heavyweight freight locomotives. The West Coast line could therefore be served by a single type of mixed traffic design capable of hauling either express passenger trains or continuously-fitted medium-speed goods services.

Proposed locomotives were to be capable of hauling a 475ton express from Manchester to Euston at an average speed of 67mph, with a maximum of 100mph and an average of 90mph on level track. They should also be capable of moving a 950ton freight train from Willesden near London to Longsight near Manchester at an average speed of 42mph and a maximum speed of 55mph and of working express freights of 500tons at an average speed of 60mph.

Within the specification there were also a number of performance requirements, one requiring that a locomotive should be capable of starting a 950ton train up to 20mph on a 1-in-100 gradient three times in a row and also that it should be capable of working the same 950ton train for ten continuous miles at a speed of 10mph – the latter requirement being to replicate the conditions under which trains were still being operated during periods when dense fog or smog blanketed the country. An alternative specification was to be applied to five additional locomotives which were to be

The Class 90s were the most modern Bo-Bo electrics to operate on the West Coast, although they have now been ousted to freight duties and express passenger work on the Great Eastern Main Line. 90004 climbs Belstead bank from Ipswich with a Norwich to Liverpool Street service on June 21 2005. Brian Stephenson.

Table 1 - Bo-Bo electric locomotives of the West Coast Main Line

Class	AL1	AL2	AL3	AL4	AL5	AL6		
TOPS Class	81	82	83	84	85	86	87	90
Numbers (first)	E3001-23 E3096/7	E3046-55	E3024-35 E3303/4 E3100	E3036-45	E3056-95	E3101-200		
TOPS	81001-22	82001-8	83001-15	84001-10	85001-40	86001-48 86101-03 86204-252	87001-35 87101	90001-50
Built	1959	1960	1960	1960	1960	1965	1973	1988
Number built	25	10	15	10	40	100	36	50
Length	56ft 6in	56ft 0in	52ft 6in	53ft 6in	56ft 6in	56ft 6in	56ft 6in	61ft 8in
HP	3,200	3,300	2,950	3,100	3,200	3,600	5,000	5,000
Traction Motors	AEI	AEI	English Electric	GEC	AEI	AEI	GEC	GEC
Max Speed	100mph	100mph	100mph	100mph	100 mph	100mph	110 mph	110mph
Wheel Arrangement	Bo-Bo	Bo-Bo	Bo-Bo	Bo-Bo	Bo-Bo	Bo-Bo	Bo-Bo	Bo-Bo
Wheel Diameter	4ft 0in	4ft 0in	4ft 0in	4ft 0in	4ft 0in	3ft 9½in	3ft 9¼in	3ft 9¼in
Max T.E.	50,000lbs	50,000lbs	38,000lbs	50,000lbs	50,000lbs	58,000lbs	58,000lbs	58,000lbs
Weight	78ton 3cwt	78ton 10cwt	75ton 4cwt	75ton 7cwt	81ton 3cwt	81ton 10 cwt	81ton 19cwt	84tons 10 cwt

Manchester Piccadilly was the first station on the West Coast Main Line to provide a terminus point for electric hauled 25kV AC trains. On September 18 1960 AL2 E3046 awaits departure time. Colour Rail.

Opposite page top: Class 87 87002 speeds through the Lune Gorge with the 4.10pm Glasgow-London Euston on August 19 1984. Les Nixon.

Opposite page bottom: An AL4 and AL1 draw to a halt at the buffer stops inside the trainshed at Manchester Piccadilly having arrived from Crewe in 1960. Colour Rail.

fitted with a different gear ratio which would allow their use on 1,250ton freight trains at a speed of 42mph.

Bo-Bo designs

Surprisingly the design called for the adoption of the Bo-Bo wheel arrangement, in which each end of the locomotive was carried on a four-wheel bogie with all axles powered. On the Sheffield-Manchester line the 26000 series EM1s were of the Bo-Bo wheel arrangement but these were predominantly intended for freight work. On the other hand the mainly-passenger EM2s of the 27000 series were equipped with Co-Co three-axle bogies to improve riding at high speed. The decision to go for the Bo-Bo was probably influenced by the outstanding success of the French BB9200 class, which was putting in impressive performances and rode no worse than the CC7100 series Co-Cos with which they shared duties.

Another influence on the design was the requirement from the civil engineer that the total weight of the locomotive, if carried on four axles, was not to exceed 80 tons with a wheel diameter of not less than 4ft 0in, something of a tall order for a locomotive which was going to have to develop around 3,300hp. By comparison the EM1s produced only 1,868hp but weighed 87.9tons and the 2,490hp EM2s weighed 102tons.

British Railways, having specified the performance levels, was now ready to place orders yet there was no experience in this country in producing locomotives of this type. As a result a detailed specification was drawn up which, surprisingly, did not draw on French experience but instead called for a

locomotive built to a completely new design on two four-wheel bogies which were to have the traction motors remotely mounted from the axles. These in turn were to be driven with flexible drives in an effort to reduce the effect the locomotives would have on the track at high speed. The motors were to be DC, with the AC current rectified within the locomotive.

Five manufacturers were offered the chance to construct to this very detailed specification, which covered such matters as diverse as mechanical layout, appearance and driving controls. The general body outline was also specified and included a very attractive three-window cab and fibre glass covers along the roof line to partially hide the dip which housed the pantographs and other equipment. To achieve the reduction in weight called for the bodies were to be built as a weight-carrying structure, abandoning the principle of having a separate chassis or frame onto which everything else would be mounted. Deep lattice girder was to be used for the sides and this was to be covered with sheet steel. The cab roofs were to be glass fibre and the controls of each type were to be the same so that drivers could move from one to the other without confusion.

The general arrangement suggested was for power collected from one of two pantographs to be passed via an air blast circuit breaker to the main transformer, which would be mounted roughly in the centre of the body. Current from this would go, at a reduced voltage, to three mercury-arc type rectifiers and from there on to the traction motors, each of which would have a continuous rating of 847 horsepower at 975 volts and 847

amperes. However manufacturers were free to pursue their own ideas as long as these could be accommodated within the basic design brief.

Contract winners

Main contractors were to be Associated Electric Industries Ltd of Rugby (with mechanical parts from Birmingham Railway Carriage & Wagon Co), Associated Electrical Industries of Manchester (with parts from Beyer Peacock), English Electric Group (mechanical parts from Vulcan Foundry), The General Electric Co (with parts from North British) and British Railways, Doncaster (with electrics from AEI, Rugby).

In all 100 locomotives were ordered to form the pilot batches and these were to become classes AL1-AL5, later to be known as Class 81-85. But with work progressing on the line itself there was an urgent need to train drivers in handling

the new traction and with this in mind
one of the two Western Region gas
turbine locomotives, 18100, was taken
to the Metropolitan Vickers works in
Stockton-on-Tees in 1958 and there it was
converted into a straight electric by
removal of the gas turbine and associated
components in exchange for a
transformer and rectifers. Two of the six
traction motors were isolated and items
such as fuel tanks were removed. Fitted
with a single pantograph and renumbered
E1000 the locomotive was despatched to
the Stockport avoiding line where it was
stabled at East Didsbury and used in the
training of drivers. The cabs were
modified from right hand drive to left
hand drive during the conversion and the
locomotive was fitted with controls
identical to those being fitted to the new
machines.

As the new locomotives began to
arrive in 1959 E1000 became quickly

redundant, though renumbered E2001 it did see periods of use at Crewe, Liverpool and Glasgow before being withdrawn in 1968 and finally scrapped in 1972.

The first of the new locomotives to be handed over, on November 27 1959, was AL1 (later Class 81) E3001 which was the prototype of 25 to come from AEI (Rugby) with mechanical components from Birmingham Railway Carriage and Wagon Co Ltd. These had low-tension tap-changer control and three six-anode mercury-arc rectifiers of a design which was then common in industry. The bogies had fixed bolsters based on an Alsthom type which pivoted on a vertical column

fitted with conical rubber bearings. Lateral movement was controlled with springs and part of the body weight was carried on side bearers. The flexible drive from the traction motors was also an Alsthom design.

In March 1960 the first of the AL4s (later Class 84) was ready. These ten locomotives had electrical equipment by the General Electric Company with mechanical components by the North British Locomotive Co. Numbered from E3036 control was by tap-changing on a high tension auto transformer while these were fitted with a specially-developed single-anode rectifier. In these locomotives the bogies were more conventional, being

of swing bolster construction and with traction and braking forces being transmitted by rubber-bushed links. The drive in this case was a Brown-Boveri/SLM type.

The third variant to take to the rails was the AL2 (later Class 82), ten examples of which were also constructed and which were numbered from E3046. The first of these was ready in May 1960, having been built by AEI (Manchester) with mechanical parts from Beyer Peacock and Co, also of Manchester. Control on these was by a chain-driven high tension tap changer while the rectifier was similar to that used on the AL1. The bogies were a development of those used previously by Beyer Peacock and allowed for the body to be carried on links suspended from the bogie frame, both ends of which carried rubber joints. This arrangement gave no metallic surfaces to wear out. The transmission again used the Alsthom design and was similar to the AL1.

Next to appear was the AL3 (later Class 83), the first of which made an appearance in July 1960. These 15 locomotives were built by English Electric and were fitted with mechanical parts from the famous Vulcan Foundry. Originally numbered E3024-3035/3303-3304/3100 the rather haphazard numbering was as a result of E3303-3305 being allocated to the locomotives geared for freight work. However E3305 was actually produced to a different specification, as E3100, and was fitted

with silicon rectifiers and low tension tap changing. The other two were later re-geared to standard configuration and then renumbered E3098/9. Class 83 was the only one of the prototypes which used three-phase motors for the auxiliaries, such as the oil and water pumps, fans and blowers. These locomotives were also fitted with ignitron rectifiers. The bogies were a type of swing bolster designed to save weight while Brown-Boveri/SLM flexible drives completed the traction package.

The final design to appear was BR's own AL5 (later Class 85), of which 40 were eventually built. These used electrical parts from AEI (Rugby) and were the first locomotives to be fitted with semi-conductor rectifiers, which were already in use in EMUs. As may be expected the electrical equipment was basically the same as the Class 82, although the class was fitted with rheostatic braking, which involved the fitting of a braking resistor inside the locomotive body. Bogie, suspension and drive arrangements were to the Alsthom design and closely followed that of the AL1.

Second generation

Following delivery of the original 100 locomotives electrification of the West Coast Main Line continued gradually on the section south of Crewe and as this progressed an order was placed for a further 100 locomotives, with the first being ready by July 1965. Designated AL6 (later Class 86) these were all to be of the same design, although construction was to be shared between British Railways at Doncaster and English Electric's Vulcan Works. Electrical equipment was to come from English Electric and AEI.

These new locomotives incorporated various changes based on experience. The tap changer was similar to that on the Class 82 but upgraded while the work of the rectifier was split into four smaller units with each traction motor having its own supply and with the control gear being likewise split – a facility which gave the locomotive a degree of redundancy should a fault occur.

However the biggest change was on the bogies where flexible drives were abandoned in favour of axle-hung traction motors, something which gave grave cause for concern when the locomotives went into service with poor riding and track damage being recurring features. Many of these locomotives were later fitted with flexicoil suspension and/or resilient wheels to try and counteract this problem and three were even rebuilt to have their traction motors remotely mounted as per the original designs.

Originally numbered from E3101 the class soon began to predominate on Euston-North West working.

When the West Coast electrification was again extended from Weaver Junction to Glasgow in 1974 British Railways needed to increase its stud of electric locomotives, leading to yet another development of the original Bo-Bo design. The first of the Class 87s (TOPs numbering now having come into force) were completed in June 1973 and saw several upgrades which increased their horsepower to a massive 5,000hp. Many features of the AL6s were continued, but not the troublesome traction motor arrangement, which reverted to being fully sprung within the bogie frames with flexible drive.

The bogies were fitted with secondary suspension with three flexicoil springs on each side and there were other improvements which were intended to improve the ride, reduce track wear and also make life easier for fitting staff. Control was by a tap changer similar to that in the Class 86 but with a higher rating and the locomotives were equipped from new with train air brakes only. Thirty-five locomotives were built and were easily identifiable by the cab, which now only had two front windows instead of three and by a lack of a four-character headcode panel. The 36th Class 87 had major differences, including thyristor power control, and was numbered 87101.

With all the Class 87s in traffic the West Coast had a formidable fleet but by the mid-1980s, and with some of the original locomotives being 25 years old, thoughts turned to building a further tranche of locomotives. Originally these were considered to be a development of the Class 87 to be known as 87/2 and were intended to replace the surviving Class 81-85 machines, some of which were in quite poor condition by this time.

However once a design was finalised there were sufficient differences for the classification to be amended and the locomotives were therefore known as Class 90s.

Many of the technical features followed the Class 87 closely, but the 90s had thyristor control, as pioneered on 87101, and a number of other improvements. British Rail Engineering at Crewe was responsible for the erection of the locomotives, the first of which appeared in 1987. With the arrival of the last in 1990 many of the earlier locomotives were withdrawn and some of the Class 86s were downgraded from top-link duties.

Bo-Bo electric locomotives reigned supreme on the West Coast line from electrification in 1959 right through to the introduction of the Pendolino multiple unit in 2001. Although all the AL1-AL5s have gone from the main line there are still a handful of AL6s engaged on freight work while the bulk of the 87s are now gainfully employed in Bulgaria. Many of the Class 90s are currently working away from their original stamping ground with services from Liverpool Street to East Anglia being dominated by the class and others are working freight trains elsewhere. Fortunately there are working examples of the AL6 and the Class 87 in preservation and there is an AL2, AL3, AL4 and AL5 to look at in Barrow Hill Roundhouse near Chesterfield as well as an 87 at Crewe Heritage Centre.

Despite initial scepticism from some quarters and a lack of design experience in the UK the use of Bo-Bo electric locomotives on high-speed services on the West Coast has been an exceptional success. While perhaps not as charismatic as other express types these electric locomotives have a huge following and interest in them will no doubt grow now that their days of dominating West Coast services are over.

Following the introduction of the tops numbering system and full yellow ends the AC electrics received standard BR blue. Class 82 82008 leads a down express at Greenholme on April 16 1981. Les Nixon

Review of the year
2009-2010

Hornby Magazine's Editor **Mike Wild** looks back over the past 12 months at the big news and releases which have shaped the ready-to-run market.

Every month exciting new models are released and announced, but the past 12 months have perhaps been the most exciting yet with more new products than ever being revealed by both manufacturers and shops.

Over the past year two things really stand out – the pace of change and improvement within the 'N' gauge ready-to-run market and, perhaps more significantly, the rise and rise of commissioned models. This latter factor has changed the way we look at the

ready-to-run market because while most of the models that have been commissioned will be produced by the well known brands of Bachmann, Dapol, Heljan and Hornby there has been a series of new announcements by retailers as exclusive commissions.

All of a sudden it seems that the potential of commissioned models has really hit home. The trend was started by Kernow Model Rail Centre and now Hattons of Liverpool, Rails of Sheffield and Olivia's Trains of Sheffield have

joined with their own announcements too.

We start this review in September 2009...

September 2009
The month starts with Bachmann's plans for a Stanier 'Black Five' and BR '4MT' 2-6-0 in 'N' gauge plus the first look at the 'N' gauge '3MT' 2-6-2T from the same company. Also revealed are a GWR 'Toad' brake van, MBA and MOA box wagons for 'N'.

In 'OO' Bachmann revealed the first pre-production shots of its eagerly awaited Robinson 'O4' 2-8-0 together with liveried samples of the BR 4-CEP EMU and Class 47/4. Hornby's new tooling for the GWR 'Castle' 4-6-0 also broke cover offering a first glimpse of the model.

Pullman modellers were treated to the release of Hornby's 'Devon Belle' observation car and Pullman bar car which complemented the already extensive range of eight-wheel Pullman cars available from Hornby. In 'N' gauge Bachmann's Class 150/2 and revised Class 37/0 also arrived offering more to choice to the modern image modeller.

October 2009

The 10th month of 2009 was busy with two high profile releases: Hornby's BR 'Clan' 4-6-2 and Heljan's model of Brush prototype HS4000 Kestrel. Both models wowed modellers with their attention to detail and high performance chassis.

In the news Dapol led the way with its plans for a LNER Thompson 'B1' 4-6-0, Class 121 railcar, HST power cars, a Class 92 and Class 142 in 'N' gauge while also revealing pre-production models of the progressing 'N' gauge Class 58 and 86.

Bachmann was also busy revealing the first pre-production shots of its LNER Peppercorn 'A2' 4-6-2 and Class 105 DMU together with liveried samples of the BR '3MT' 2-6-2T

November 2009

The Warley National Model Railway Exhibition provided the perfect platform for Bachmann to release the first versions of its BR 4-CEP EMU and BR '3MT'

Hornby launched its BR 'Clan' 4-6-2 in October 2009.

Heljan followed up its popular model of Brush prototype D0280 *Falcon* with this superb model of HS4000 *Kestrel*.

The National Railway Museum teamed up with Bachmann to produce this spectacular model of GWR 'City' 4-4-0 3440 *City of Truro* in 'OO'.

2-6-2T. The 4-CEP represented a huge step forward in ready-to-run equipment by becoming the first four-car third-rail EMU to be produced in 'OO'.

Concurrently Hornby also released its Hitachi Class 395 'Javelin' EMU in 'OO' while Lionheart Trains launched its DCC sound fitted GWR '64XX' and '74XX' 0-6-0PTs.

In 'N' gauge Dapol's Class 153 DMU made its debut offering another well thought out multiple unit.

Announcements during November were significant. Bachmann revealed

it would produce the new Freightliner 'Powerhaul' Class 70 following granting of an exclusive license by Freightliner while Danish manufacturer Heljan announced its models of the English Electric 'Baby Deltic' Class 23, BRCW prototype D0260 *Lion* plus Waggon und Maschinenbau, Park Royal and AC Cars railbuses in 'OO'. An 'O' gauge model of the English Electric 'Deltic' was also announced by Heljan in November.

In 'N' gauge Bachmann revealed that the Class 14 would be reproduced in 'N'

gauge at the annual Warley National Model Railway Exhibition while Kernow Model Rail Centre commissioned the PBA and JIA china clay wagons from Dapol in 'OO' too.

December 2009

The surprise announcement of the year was the Bachmann/National Railway Museum model of GWR 'City' 4-4-0 3440 *City of Truro* as a ready-to-run model in 'OO'. This second commission from the NRM followed in the footsteps of the prototype Deltic model and it was revealed to the model media on December 4 at the Gloucestershire Warwickshire Railway.

The GWR fared well during the month as Hornby also released the first versions of its highly anticipated GWR 'Castle' 4-6-0 together with its sound-fitted Gresley 'A4' 4-6-2 and Stanier 'Black Five' 4-6-0. Bachmann also released its first revised Class 47/4 models in 'OO' during the month.

In 'N' gauge Bachmann's new model of the BR Sulzer Class 24 also arrived setting new standards for the company's 'N' gauge diesel locomotives under the Graham Farish brand.

The annual Hornby media day revealed the shape of things to come in 2010 when Hornby announced it would be producing new versions of the GWR '28XX' 2-8-0 and LNER 'B17' 4-6-0 plus an 'L1' 2-6-4T for steam followers. These were backed up by a range of new liveries on existing steam models plus plans for a model of the third-rail BR 4-VEP EMU, more DCC sound fitted locomotives including the GWR 'Castle' 4-6-0, SR 'Schools' 4-4-0 and BR Class 08 diesel shunter. Rolling stock announcements included a new range of Western Region Hawksworth coaches plus KFA container flats and OTA timber wagons all for 'OO'.

January 2010

The highlight of January was the arrival of Hattons exclusive 'OO' model of the BR

New locomotive announcements 2009-2010		
Model	**Scale**	**Manufacturer**
Stanier 'Black Five' 4-6-0	'N'	Bachmann Graham Farish
BR '4MT' 2-6-0	'N'	Bachmann Graham Farish
LNER Thompson 'B1' 4-6-0	'N'	Dapol
Class 92	'N'	Dapol
Class 121	'N'	Dapol
Class 43 (HST power cars)	'N'	Dapol
Class 142	'N'	Dapol
Class 70	'OO'/'N'	Bachmann
Class 23	'OO'	Heljan
BRCW D0260 *Lion*	'OO'	Heljan
Waggon und Maschinenbau railbus	'OO'	Heljan
Park Royal railbus	'OO'	Heljan
AC Cars railbus	'OO'	Heljan
Class 55	'O'	Heljan
Class 14	'N'	Bachmann Graham Farish
GWR '28XX' 2-8-0	'OO'	Hornby
LNER 'L1' 2-6-4T	'OO'	Hornby
LNER 'B17' 4-6-0	'OO'	Hornby
BR 4-VEP EMU	'OO'	Hornby
Fowler '7F' 2-8-0	'OO'	Bachmann
Midland '3F' 0-6-0	'OO'	Bachmann
Derby Lightweight DMU	'OO'	Bachmann
Class 85	'OO'	Bachmann
Class 350 Desiro	'OO'	Bachmann
Prototype Deltic	'N'	Bachmann Graham Farish
EM1 Bo-Bo	'OO'	Olivia's Trains/Heljan
EM2 Co-Co	'OO'	Olivia's Trains/Heljan
LMS 10000/10001	'OO'	Rails of Sheffield/Bachmann
Class 28	'OO'	Hattons/Heljan
Class 143/144	'OO'	Realtrack Models
LMS 10000/10001	'OO'	Hattons/Dapol
Blue Pullman DEMU (Midland set)	'OO'	Bachmann
LSWR 'O2' 0-4-4T	'OO'	Kernow MRC/Dapol
Bulleid 1-Co-Co-1 10201-10203	'OO'	Kernow MRC/Dapol

Class 14 hydraulic. This locomotive essentially proved the potential of commissioned models with the first batch selling out within a couple of months.

January also saw Electrifying Trains launch its 'O' gauge model of the Southern Railway designed 2-BIL EMU while Bachmann released its revised Class 47/4 in 'N' gauge. Also debuting was OO Works SECR 'H' 0-4-4T offering Southern modellers another choice of small passenger tank.

In the news *Hornby Magazine* launched its limited edition model of ex-Stratford Depot Class 47 47572 *Ely Cathedral* in BR large logo blue while Bachmann revealed liveried pre-production models of its Class 03 diesel shunter.

February 2010

'O' gauge modellers received a boost in February with the release of Heljan's 'O' gauge Class 20 offering a fourth ready-to-run model from the Danish manufacturer in 7mm scale. Also released was Hornby's DCC sound fitted Class 50 plus a range of reliveries on existing models.

Hornby Magazine's LMS Stove R six-wheel passenger brake model also got off the ground as Dapol started work on the CAD/CAM drawing work plus Bachmann revealed the first painted samples of its 'N' gauge Stanier 'Black Five' 4-6-0. Heljan was busy completing the first pre-production samples of its Class 15 and Class 86 for 'OO' as well as displaying progress on its 'O' gauge Class 33.

Hornby released its model of the Class 395 high-speed EMU in November 2009 just after the opening of the second phase of the Channel Tunnel Rail Link.

March 2010

The third month of 2010 started with Bachmann revealing its 2010 catalogue which contained five new ready-to-run models covering the Fowler '7F' 2-8-0, Midland '3F' 0-6-0, Derby Lightweight DMU, Class 85 overhead electric and Siemens Class 350 Desiro overhead EMU for 'OO'

In 'N' gauge it revealed that the prototype Deltic would be reproduced together with a range of brand new Mk 1 carriages to take over from the aging Graham Farish printed versions.

Dapol's new 'N' gauge Class 153s followed the high standards laid down by its Class 156s in early 2009.

Heljan's BTH Class 15 showed the potential of pilot scheme diesels as ready-to-run models.

The company also took the opportunity to display the latest samples of its 'Black Five', BR '4MT', BR '3MT' and Class 14 models in 'N' gauge together with its 'OO' Class 105 samples.

Kernow Model Rail Centre hit the news again with its change from Dapol to Bachmann for production of its Southern Region Class 205 Diesel Electric Multiple Unit (DEMU) which now included a sound-fitted version.

Hornby was also busy and launched an additional batch of new releases for its 2010 programme including LNER 'A4' 2509 *Silver Link* to mark the 75th anniversary of the iconic 'Silver Jubilee' train plus new versions of its Gresley 'A3', Bulleid rebuilt 'Merchant Navy', DCC ready models of the 'J83' and 'J52' and new coaches. The N Gauge Society revealed it would be working with Dapol to produce an exclusive model of the BR independent snowplough for 'N' gauge modellers.

New releases during March were headlined by Heljan with its stunning model of the BTH Class 15 touching down together with the promised 'OO' gauge Class 86. Bachmann released its DCC sound fitted Stanier 'Jubilee' 4-6-0 too, while Heljan scored a third hit with its new 'O' gauge Mk 1 carriages. Completing the bulging line-up of new models were Hornby's new Mk 3 DVT, an upgraded version of the Class 42 'Warship' from Bachmann with directional lighting and a 21-pin decoder socket and Dapol's new 'N' gauge Class 86.

April 2010

For the second year running the Blue Pullman DEMU topped with annual British Model Railway Wish List Poll in 2010 beating a range of popular steam locomotives to the top. Highlights amongst the top ten most wanted models included the GNR 'J6' 0-6-0 and Caledonian Railway '439' 0-4-4T as well as the 'D11' 4-4-0, Brighton 'H2' 4-4-2 and original 'Merchant Navy'.

New releases were headlined by the arrival of Hornby's 'Bournemouth Belle' train pack featuring the brand new 12-wheel Pullman cars announced in the company's 2010 catalogue and packaged

New locomotive releases 2009-2010		
Model	Scale	Manufacturer
Class 150/2	'N'	Bachmann Graham Farish
Class 37/0 (revised)	'N'	Bachmann Graham Farish
Brush HS4000 *Kestrel*	'OO'	Heljan
BR 'Clan' 4-6-2	'OO'	Hornby
BR 4-CEP EMU	'OO'	Bachmann
BR '3MT' 2-6-2T	'OO'	Bachmann
Hitachi Class 395	'OO'	Hornby
GWR '64XX' and '74XX' 0-6-0PT	'O'	Lionheart Trains
Class 153	'N'	Dapol
GWR 'City' 4-4-0	'OO'	NRM/Bachmann
GWR 'Castle' 4-6-0	'OO'	Hornby
Sound fitted LNER 'A4' 4-6-2	'OO'	Hornby
Sound fitted LMS 'Black Five' 4-6-0	'OO'	Hornby
Class 24	'N'	Bachmann Graham Farish
Class 47/4	'OO'	Bachmann
Class 14	'OO'	Hattons/Heljan
SR 2-BIL EMU	'O'	Electrifying Trains
Class 47/4	'N'	Bachmann Graham Farish
SECR 'H' 0-4-4T	'OO'	OO Works
Class 20	'O'	Heljan
Sound fitted Class 50	'OO'	Hornby
Class 15	'OO'	Heljan
Class 86	'OO'	Heljan
Class 86	'N'	Dapol
Sound fitted Stanier 'Jubilee' 4-6-0	'OO'	Bachmann
LMS Stanier 'Black Five' 4-6-0	'N'	Bachmann Graham Farish
GWR 'Manor' 4-6-0	'N'	Ixion Models
Robinson 'O4' 2-8-0	'OO'	Bachmann
Class 58	'N'	Dapol
BR '4MT' 2-6-0	'N'	Bachmann Graham Farish
Class 108 (three-car)	'N'	Bachmann Graham Farish
'Brighton Belle' 5-BEL EMU	'OO'	Golden Age Models
Class 105 DMU	'OO'	Bachmann
BR '3MT' 2-6-2T	'N'	Bachmann Graham Farish
GWR '28XX' 2-8-0	'OO'	Hornby
Sound fitted GWR 'Castle' 4-6-0	'OO'	Hornby

Bachmann wowed branch line modellers with this superb model of the BR '3MT' 2-6-2T.

with BR 'Britannia' 70009 *Alfred the Great* – the locomotive which worked the train regularly in 1951.

In 'N' gauge Bachmann released the all new 'N' gauge Stanier 'Black Five' in the Graham Farish range offering a highly detailed and high performance model of this popular prototype. It was joined by an equally high profile model – Ixion Models Mk II GWR 'Manor' 4-6-0, a model which featured some neat tricks and wonderful details.

May 2010

Bachmann launched the first all new 'OO' steam locomotive model of the year in May in the shape of its eagerly anticipated Robinson 'O4' 2-8-0. This model, which had scored highly on wish lists for several years, filled a huge gap in ready-to-run Eastern Region models and offered performance and detail to boot.

Dapol also released the first of its superb new 'N' gauge Class 58 models while the same company also launched its KQA pocket wagons in 'OO' gauge and Silver Bullet china clay wagons in 'N'. Bachmann's Graham Farish range grew with release of the all new BR '4MT' 2-6-0 and the three-car Class 108 DMUs, BDA bolster wagon and GWR 'Toad' brake vans too. During May Hornby released its new coaling tower from the Skaledale range, although the imposing structure was limited to 600 models only.

However, the new releases were somewhat overshadowed by a series of announcements from Olivia's Trains, Rails of Sheffield and Hattons. Olivia's Trains announced that it would be working with Heljan to produce exclusive models of the Blue Pullman DEMU and Woodhead overhead electric EM1 Bo-Bo and EM2 Co-Co. Rails of Sheffield revealed its plans to produce exclusive models of LMS prototypes 10000 and 10001 with Bachmann and Hattons announced it would make the Metrovick Co-Bo (Class 28) in an exclusive deal with Heljan.

Elsewhere Bachmann revealed the first pre-production model of its

Hornby's first all new model of 2010 was the GWR '28XX' 2-8-0 – a model which offers wonderful detail.

The all new Hornby GWR 'Castle' arrived in December 2009 offering a highly detailed version of a popular model.

The Bachmann Class 105 DMU arrived in July creating a new opportunity for transition era modellers.

Freightliner 'Powerhaul' Class 70 and Fowler '7F' 2-8-0 while Dapol revealed the first CAD/CAM drawings for its promised 'N' gauge HST power cars.

June 2010

The undoubted highlight of the month was the arrival of Golden Age Models stunning replica of the 'Brighton Belle' 5-BEL EMU in 'OO' gauge. Costing a cool £1,995 this superb model offered everything and more including full DCC fitment from the factory, interior detail and working table lamps.

Also making it to the shops during June were Modelzone's specially

commissioned models of the BR Travelling Post Office (POS) vans in 'OO' plus Dapol's new 'Megafret' twinsets, DCC Concepts Cobalt point motors and Bachmann's MOA low-sided Megabox wagons.

In the news Bachmann showed off the first pre-production sample of its BR 2-EPB EMU while Hornby also had the first shots of its BR 4-VEP EMU to show too. *Hornby Magazine's* LMS Stove R passenger brake was cleared for work to start on the tooling following completion of CAD/CAM drawing while Kernow Model Rail Centre was also able to show the final

Hattons proved that commissioned models work with the release of its Heljan produced Class 14 in 'OO'.

drawings for its Beattie 2-4-0WT before production of the tools started and similarly Dapol completed the drawing work for its 'OO' gauge Class 22.

Dapol made a series of surprise 'OO' gauge announcements at the DEMU Showcase covering instantly available models of the IOA and JNA Network Rail ballast wagons plus the start of work on a models of the 'Turbot' spoil wagon, BBA bogie steel coil wagon and MRA five vehicle side tipping ballast wagon.

Another surprise announcement was the revelation that Dapol would be releasing 'OO' catenary masts following the success of its 'N' gauge versions.

A new name entered the ready-to-run market too as Realtrack models revealed its plans to produce the Class 143/144 DMUs in 'OO' gauge and the latest progress on its FLA container flat twin sets.

July 2010

Despite summer normally being a quiet period, July was the complete opposite with two highly significant announcements and two high profile releases.

Hattons of Liverpool revealed in a surprise announcement that it would be working with Dapol to produce exclusive models of LMS twin 10000 and 10001 in 'OO' just two months after Rails of Sheffield had revealed its project with Bachmann.

Bachmann too was busy with the company launching its own 'OO' gauge Blue Pullman project at its annual open day. Bachmann's Blue Pullman saw Olivia's Trains shelve its plans to produce the train. Also revealed were the latest samples of the Fowler '7F' 2-8-0, Railtrack MPV, Railtrack Autoballaster wagons and LNER/BR box vans in 'OO' together with

decorated samples of the new range of BR Mk I carriages for 'N' gauge. Dapol also cleared its high specification BR 'Britannia' 4-6-0 for production in 'N' gauge and revealed the first pictures of its 'N' gauge Thompson 'B1' 4-6-0.

New releases were lead by the arrival of Bachmann's stunning Cravens Class 105 DMU – the first of the two-car power twin sets arrived during the month for 'OO'. Other highlights included Bachmann's Graham Farish BR '3MT' 2-6-2T in 'N' gauge and the JPA bulk cement wagon in 'OO'.

August 2010

The GWR was in favour again during August with Hornby releasing the first of its brand new GWR Churchward '28XX'

One of the latest releases is Dapol's new BR 'Britannia' 4-6-2 – a model which raised the bar for 'N' gauge steam outline products.

2-8-0s which were to be followed soon after by the Collett '2884' 2-8-0s with side window cabs. This impressive model became Hornby's first all new steam model of 2010.

Adding further to the GWR theme Hornby's DCC sound fitted 'Castle' 4-6-0 carrying the identity of 4098 *Kidwelly Castle* in BR green touched down. Also new from Hornby were the latest pair of Gresley 'A4s' in its Commonwealth Collection (60009 *Union of South Africa* and 60010 *Dominion of Canada*) while Dapol wowed the 'N' gauge market with its sublime model of the BR 'Britannia' 4-6-2 which featured a range of new and improved features for the scale.

In the news Kernow Model Rail Centre hit the headlines with the announcement of a LSWR 'O2' 0-4-4T and Bulleid designed 1-Co-Co-1 10201-10203 for 'OO' following the pre-order successes with its Beattie 2-4-0WT and D600 'Warship' models.

Rails of Sheffield confirmed that it would continue with its project to produce 10000/10001 in 'OO' with Bachmann while the company behind the Parry People Mover revealed that they were working on an 'N' gauge model of their own product.

Hornby Magazine's opinion

The past 12 months have been some of the most exciting for the hobby. Never before have so many new models been announced and commissioned and it is encouraging to see the hobby go from strength to strength.

In our view the new market for

commissioned models has driven the hobby in a new direction and one which allows us to get the models we want quicker than many would have expected. Add to this the fact that few could have predicted so many prototype diesels would be produced and it creates a blossoming picture of enticing and exciting prospects.

Standards of detail and performance continue to rise as modellers demand more on both counts and we can say from the samples received in the *Hornby Magazine* office that this level of quality really is on the up.

Our own highlights must include the

National Railway Museum/Bachmann models of GWR 'City' 3440 *City of Truro* – a truly wonderful and unexpected model – plus the announcement of the Blue Pullman and the LMS twins in 'OO' gauge. In 'N' gauge the undoubted star in our eyes in the Dapol 'Britannia' – a ground breaking model which has again shown just how much potential the scale holds.

With so many models on the cards for release in the next 12 months the *Hornby Magazine* editorial is itching to see what the future holds and you can rest assured that as soon as we have sight of the new releases our full reviews will be published in *Hornby Magazine*.

Bachmann released its eagerly anticipated Robinson 'O4' 2-8-0 in May.

Golden Age Models wowed 'OO' modellers with its stunning replica of the 5-BEL EMU.

Diesel
decades

The current railway scene isn't to be ignored and it continues to flourish as a subject for modellers. Here we take a look at our top five modern traction layouts featuring the 1980s, 1990s and 2000s.

Widnes Vine Yard

Widnes Vine Yard started with the burning desire to create a main line railway model, but you might not expect that the original ideas floated by the Wirral Finescale Railway Modellers were for a steam era project set on the West Coast Main Line with ideals such as fog working with dry ice!

However, what ensued was nothing of the sort. The project developed and moved to a 1970s setting based around the signalbox named Widnes No. 1 on the former St Helens Railway from Widnes to St Helens and later moved to the current railway scene and what you see before you.

Widnes Vine Yard has now been on the exhibition circuit in one form or another for 10 years and has built up a reputation for quality operation which is in no small part due to the Digital Command Control and computer technology used to operate the trains. This includes computer signalling, route setting and automatic train selection at random through a piece of software developed by Mike Turner.

Widnes Vine Yard statistics	
Owner:	Wirral Finescale Railway Modellers
Scale:	'OO'
Length:	23ft
Width:	9ft
Track:	Peco code 75
Layout type:	Continuous run
Period:	2000-2010
Featured:	HM38

The layout itself is a fine representation of modern life and captures both the clinical nature of today's railway routes as well as the cluttered embankments, modern street fittings and other peripheral items such as industrial units, all of which play their part in making Widnes Vine Yard so impressive.

The group behind Widnes Vine Yard also spend much time researching and developing new train formations for the layout and, as with today's railway network, new liveries are quickly added to the fleet together with new formations as additional rolling stock options become available.

This, then, is Widnes Vine Yard.

Opposite page: Freightliner Shanks liveried 66522 works its way across the main lines with a bulk cement working. Mike Wild.

With a long rake of engineers wagons behind EWS Class 60 60021 takes the branch route at Widnes Vine Yard. Mike Wild.

A Class 57/3 hauls a failed Voyager DEMU through Widnes Vine Yard to Central Rivers Depot for remedial work. Mike Wild.

A detailed and weathered Lima Class 33 stands between the platforms of Walford Town awaiting departure. Mike Wild.

Walford Town

This 'EM' gauge layout started life in 1985 and at the time it was based on current railway operations followed by members of the Leamington and Warwick Model Railway Society. The real railway has moved on, but Walford Town has remained firmly rooted in the late 1980s and its overall feel and rolling stock reflect this to this day.

The late 1980s were chosen as an alternative to the 'usual' club layouts featuring BR 1950s period steam operations and it also opened the doors to working in a new scale for many – that being 18mm gauge, 'EM', track. This also allowed new members to acquire new skills from those already seasoned in track construction and rolling stock modification.

The terminus station is set in the East of London and is a fictitious location on the former Great Eastern Railway network.

Originally it was planned to depict BR rail blue formations, but by following the changes on BR during the mid to late 1980s it became clear that much more variety in terms of liveries was available to the modeller of the time.

As the layout developed the stock grew to include Network SouthEast and Railfreight grey and red stripe liveried locomotives as well as the latest air-braked wagons which were becoming more commonplace on the network.

All this adds up to a convincing and now historic piece of modelling which captures a period now long passed. Building upon this further are the road vehicles and, perhaps most notably, the Texas DIY store located above the stained brick retaining wall behind the station.

This layout remains part of the Leamington and Warwick Model Railway Society's exhibition roster after a return to the circuit in 2009.

Walford Town statistics

Owner:	Leamington and Warwick Model Railway Society
Scale:	4mm ('EM' gauge)
Length:	20ft
Width:	3ft 6in
Track:	Handbuilt
Period:	Great Eastern, 1984-1988
Featured:	HM31

A pair of Class 20s rest
between duties in the
locomotive stabling line.
Mike Wild.

A detailed and modified Graham Farish Class 33 takes the single line junction above Stoney Lane Depot as a 4-VEP EMU overtakes.

Chris Nevard.

Stoney Lane Depot

Stoney Lane Depot is set in the Network SouthEast era (1986-2000), although you'll see slightly older and newer road vehicles, railway stock and dated artefacts used, and is located in South London around the Southwark area.

All the structures are scratch built and most are based on real buildings from around South London such as Battersea, Croydon, Surbiton, Borough, Stewarts Lane and Victoria.

The main lines are on typical inner city viaducts that span the Thames flood plain as they reach the great Southern termini. Below them is a small depot and Electric Multiple Unit (EMU) stabling point loosely based on Stewarts Lane. Operations consist of typical EMU commuter trains

with cross-London freight making it a busy layout.

The layout was built as a bigger and better replacement for Graham's earlier Hedges Hill Cutting effort and to hopefully showcase the improvements in standards and quality that have been occurring in 'N' gauge in recent years. These include Peco's finer scale code 55

track, the latest finer profile blackened wheels to NMRA standards and some of the latest kits and ready-to-run stock being produced.

It is hoped that it demonstrates what is achievable in 'N' gauge with commercially available products and standards, without the need to completely scratch build track and stock to 2mm finescale standards.

Stoney Lane Depot statistics	
Owner:	Graham Hedges
Scale:	'N'
Length:	8ft
Width:	2ft 6in
Track:	Peco code 55
Period:	South East, 1986-2000
Featured:	HM30

An overview of the depot and stabling point showing how the multi-level nature of Stoney Lane works. Chris Nevard.

Capturing more modern times a pair of Class 92 electrics arrive at the depot as a Network SouthEast liveried 4-CIG EMU passes on the viaduct above. Chris Nevard.

An EWS Class 08 shunts a single wagon load of steel plate at Peter Street.
Chris Nevard.

DRS 37261 draws into Peter Street with a Network Rail test train.
Chris Nevard.

Peter Street

Peter Harvey's Peter Street is the ultimate in compact layouts. It measures just 8ft x 1ft and conveys the impression of a suburban terminus set in the West Midlands.

It is built to 'OO' scale and makes the most of Digital Command Control for operation of the trains. Like Peter's previous layout, Dudley Road, Peter Street uses the present-day railway as its focus offering the opportunity to run a mixture of DMUs as well as locomotives in a multitude of colour schemes.

Construction began during 2008 and the basic design consists of a two-road platform and a freight siding. Two roads from the fiddle yard also extend onto the scenic section allowing locomotives and rolling stock to remain on view even when they aren't in use which allows the public to see a little more at exhibitions.

Despite its compact size the railway element is feature-packed. Working signals interlocked with the points are an impressive part of the construction together with a fully illuminated station, scratch built buildings and a neatly made concrete faced platform – all of which add to the atmosphere and period setting of Peter Street.

Peter Street has provided much enjoyment and entertainment due to the large number of movements which are possible within the compact track plan.

As a layout it shows just how much potential a present-day terminus can offer to the modeller, especially with so many attractive and finely detailed items of rolling stock becoming available.

Peter Street statistics	
Owner:	Peter Harvey
Scale:	'OO'
Length:	8ft
Width:	1ft
Track:	Peco code 75
Period:	2007-2009
Featured:	HM27

In the shadows of Hendre Lane depot 37411 *Ty Hafan* waits for its next call of duty in the cold night air. Marc Smith.

Coal sector liveried 37698 *Coedbach* shunts engineers' wagons outside the stabling point. Marc Smith.

Hendre Lane

Diesel depots are a popular type of layout and Marc Smith built Hendre Lane stabling point as a quick project to try out digital sound locomotives. The result is an atmospheric slice of South Wales railway which can be operated in a number of different periods depending upon Marc's mood.

The diesel depot wasn't Marc's first idea, but the potential for short trains within a restricted footprint won the day. Rather than opt for off-the-shelf buildings all those on Hendre Lane are scratch built and by reducing the number of buildings it is easy to transport the layout from the 1970s through to the present-day.

The whole project has been designed with realism in mind. Plans were drawn out full size on wallpaper to allow rolling stock to be positioned and moved around to check clearances and siding lengths while building mock-ups helped an appreciation of how the final format would look. The depot building is loosely based on Hither Green on the Southern Region, but with subtle modifications and weathering to capture a run-down atmosphere it suited the location well.

Digital Command Control plays an important part in Hendre Lane both in terms of operation and sound fitted locomotives. However, to increase the atmosphere a CD of background noises is played when the layout is exhibited which includes birdsong, cows, shunting sounds and more. These sounds have been acquired from various sources and amalgamated to create the finished sound file. Adding further to this wonderful atmosphere is the option to run the layout in day or night setting. Daylight illumination is through a small low energy strip light while for night time running the lighting installed on the layout from Express Models is all that is required.

As a quick project Hendre Lane shows just how much potential a compact diesel depot holds both for modelling and operation.

Hendre Lane statistics	
Owner:	Marc Smith
Scale:	'OO'
Length:	42in
Width:	15in
Track:	Peco code 75
Period:	Western Region, 1980-2000
Featured:	HM26

In work stained condition a split headcode Class 37 shunts a 'Shark' ballast plough in the yard.
Marc Smith.

FREE Binder or Slipcase
When you subscribe today

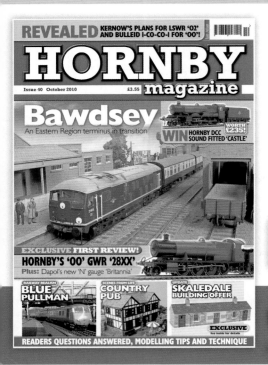